TEACHER'S PET PUBLICATIONS

LITPLAN TEACHER PACK
for
The Adventures of Tom Sawyer
based on the book by
Mark Twain

Written by
Mary B. Collins

© 1996 Teacher's Pet Publications
All Rights Reserved

This **LitPlan** for Mark Twain's
The Adventures of Tom Sawyer
has been brought to you by Teacher's Pet Publications, Inc.

Copyright Teacher's Pet Publications 1996
11504 Hammock Point
Berlin MD 21811

Only the student materials in this unit plan (such as worksheets, study questions, and tests) may be reproduced multiple times for use in the purchaser's classroom.

For any additional copyright questions,
contact Teacher's Pet Publications.

www.tpet.com

TABLE OF CONTENTS - *The Adventures of Tom Sawyer*

Introduction	6
Unit Objectives	8
Reading Assignment Sheet	9
Unit Outline	10
Study Questions (Short Answer)	13
Quiz/Study Questions (Multiple Choice)	23
Pre-reading Vocabulary Worksheets	43
Lesson One (Introductory Lesson)	57
Nonfiction Assignment Sheet	61
Oral Reading Evaluation Form	63
Writing Assignment 1	69
Writing Assignment 2	71
Writing Assignment 3	78
Writing Evaluation Form	79
Vocabulary Review Activities	73
Extra Writing Assignments/Discussion ?s	75
Unit Review Activities	81
Unit Tests	85
Unit Resource Materials	121
Vocabulary Resource Materials	135

A FEW NOTES ABOUT THE AUTHOR
Mark Twain

TWAIN, Mark (1835-1910). A onetime printer and Mississippi River boat pilot, Mark Twain became one of America's greatest authors. His 'Tom Sawyer', 'Huckleberry Finn', and 'Life on the Mississippi' rank high on any list of great American books.

Mark Twain was born Samuel Langhorne Clemens on Nov. 30, 1835, in the small town of Florida, Mo. He was the fourth of five children. His father was a hard worker but a poor provider. The family moved to Hannibal, Mo., on the Mississippi, when young Clemens was 4 years old. It was in this river town that he grew up, and from it he gathered the material for his most famous stories. The character of Judge Carpenter is somewhat like his father; Aunt Polly, his mother; Sid Sawyer, his brother Henry; Huck Finn, a town boy named Tom Blankenship; and Tom Sawyer, a combination of several boys-including himself.

His father died when he was 12, and the boy was apprenticed to a printer. An apprentice works for someone in order to learn a trade. This was the first step toward his career as a writer. In 1857 he apprenticed himself to a riverboat pilot. He became a licensed pilot and spent two and a half years at his new trade. The river swarmed with traffic, and the pilot was the most important man aboard the boat. He wrote of these years in 'Life on the Mississippi'.

The Civil War ended his career as a pilot. Clemens went west to Nevada and soon became a reporter on the Virginia City newspaper. Here he began using the pen name Mark Twain. It is an old river term meaning two fathoms, or 12 feet (4 meters), of water depth.

In 1864 he went to California. The next year he wrote his 'Jumping Frog' story, which ran in many newspapers. He was sent to the Sandwich Islands (now Hawaii) as a roving reporter, and on his return he began lecturing. He was soon on a tour of the Mediterranean and the Holy Land. From this came 'The Innocents Abroad', which made him famous.

In 1870 he married Olivia Langdon, daughter of a wealthy businessman of Elmira, N.Y. Olivia modified Twain's exaggerations, sometimes weakening his writings, sometimes actually making them more readable. They had three daughters.

Twain began turning out a new book every few years. William Dean Howells, editor of the Atlantic Monthly and a highly respected novelist, became his close friend and literary adviser.

Twain bought a publishing firm in Hartford, Conn. He earned much money writing, lecturing, and in his publishing house, but he spent it on high living and unsuccessful investments. He lost a fortune promoting a typesetting machine. By 1894 his publishing company had failed and he was bankrupt.

Twain set out on a world lecture tour to retrieve his fortune, and by 1898 his debts were paid. In his last years he traveled and spoke much but wrote comparatively little. He died on April 21, 1910.

Twain was more than a humorist. Behind his mask of humor lay a serious view of life. Tragedy had entered his own life in the poverty and early death of his father, the loss of a daughter, and his bankruptcy. His short story, 'The Man That Corrupted Hadleyburg', published in 1900, which showed greed at work in a small town, is an indication of Twain's dark side.

The controversial 'Huckleberry Finn', which is periodically banned in schools or libraries because of alleged racial overtones, can be read by children, but it is not a child's book. It has elements of heartbreak and wisdom that can be appreciated best by adults. On the other hand, 'Tom Sawyer' is primarily a juvenile book but one that can be read with pleasure by adults.

Twain's chief works are: 'The Celebrated Jumping Frog of Calaveras County', a collection published in 1867; 'The Innocents Abroad' (1869); 'Roughing It' (1872); 'The Gilded Age'-with Charles Dudley Warner (1873); 'The Adventures of Tom Sawyer' (1876); 'A Tramp Abroad' (1880); 'The Prince and the Pauper' (1882); 'Life on the Mississippi' (1883); 'The Adventures of Huckleberry Finn' (1884); 'A Connecticut Yankee in King Arthur's Court' (1889); 'The Tragedy of Pudd'nhead Wilson' (1894); and 'Personal Recollections of Joan of Arc' (1896). Printed posthumously were: 'The Mysterious Stranger' (1916); 'Mark Twain's Notebook' (1935); and 'Autobiography' (1959).

---- Courtesy of Compton's Learning Company

INTRODUCTION

This unit has been designed to develop students' reading, writing, thinking, and language skills through exercises and activities related to *The Adventures of Tom Sawyer* by Mark Twain. It includes twenty-one lessons, supported by extra resource materials.

The **introductory lessons** introduce students to the **reading project assignment** in which students prepare to act out some of the more dramatic scenes from the novel. Students are also given the materials they will be using during the unit. Students then begin the pre-reading work for the first reading assignment.

The **reading assignments** are approximately thirty pages each; some are a little shorter while others are a little longer. Students have approximately 15 minutes of pre-reading work to do prior to each reading assignment. This pre-reading work involves reviewing the study questions for the assignment and doing some vocabulary work for 8 to 10 vocabulary words they will encounter in their reading.

The **study guide questions** are fact-based questions; students can find the answers to these questions right in the text. These questions come in two formats: short answer or multiple choice. The best use of these materials is probably to use the short answer version of the questions as study guides for students (since answers will be more complete), and to use the multiple choice version for occasional quizzes. If your school has the appropriate machinery, it might be a good idea to make transparencies of your answer keys for the overhead projector.

The **vocabulary work** is intended to enrich students' vocabularies as well as to aid in the students' understanding of the book. Prior to each reading assignment, students will complete a two-part worksheet for approximately 8 to 10 vocabulary words in the upcoming reading assignment. Part I focuses on students' use of general knowledge and contextual clues by giving the sentence in which the word appears in the text. Students are then to write down what they think the words mean based on the words' usage. Part II nails down the definitions of the words by giving students dictionary definitions of the words and having students match the words to the correct definitions based on the words' contextual usage. Students should then have an understanding of the words when they meet them in the text.

After each reading assignment, students will go back and formulate answers for the study guide questions. Discussion of these questions serves as a **review** of the most important events and ideas presented in the reading assignments.

After students complete reading the work, there is a **vocabulary review** lesson which pulls together all of the fragmented vocabulary lists for the reading assignments and gives students a review of all of the words they have studied.

A lesson is devoted to the **extra discussion questions/writing assignments**. These questions focus on interpretation, critical analysis and personal response, employing a variety of thinking skills and adding to the students' understanding of the novel.

There is a second **class project** in which students plan and carry out an old-fashioned country picnic complete with food and activities.

There are three **writing assignments** in this unit, each with the purpose of informing, persuading, or having students express personal opinions. The first assignment is to express personal opinions: students are given a choice between living in our world today or living in the Midwest in the 1840s and are asked to write a composition in which they explain which they would choose and why they would choose it. The second assignment is to persuade: students pretend to be any character in the book except Huck Finn. The assignment is to write a letter to Huck convincing him to live with the Widow Douglas and become civilized. They may use any arguments except the one Tom used in the book. The third assignment is to inform: students write a composition in which they tell about the nonfiction article they have read relating to *Tom Sawyer*. This assignment is in preparation for the oral presentation they will have to make on the same topic.

As mentioned, there is a **nonfiction reading assignment**. Students are required to read a piece of nonfiction related in some way to *The Adventures of Tom Sawyer*. After reading their nonfiction pieces, students will fill out a worksheet on which they answer questions regarding facts, interpretation, criticism, and personal opinions. During one class period, students make **oral presentations** about the nonfiction pieces they have read. This not only exposes all students to a wealth of information, it also gives students the opportunity to practice **public speaking**.

The **review lesson** pulls together all of the aspects of the unit. The teacher is given four or five choices of activities or games to use which all serve the same basic function of reviewing all of the information presented in the unit.

The **unit test** comes in two formats: multiple choice or short answer. As a convenience, two different tests for each format have been included. There is also an advanced short answer test for students who need more of a challenge.

There are additional **support materials** included with this unit. The **extra activities section** includes suggestions for an in-class library, crossword and word search puzzles related to the novel, and extra vocabulary worksheets. There is a list of **bulletin board ideas** which gives the teacher suggestions for bulletin boards to go along with this unit. In addition, there is a list of **extra class activities** the teacher could choose from to enhance the unit or as a substitution for an exercise the teacher might feel is inappropriate for his/her class. **Answer keys** are located directly after the **reproducible student materials** throughout the unit. The student materials may be reproduced for use in the teacher's classroom.

UNIT OBJECTIVES - *The Adventures of Tom Sawyer*

1. To expose students to a different era of American life, prior to the Civil War and prior to the arrival of the industrial revolution to the Midwest.

2. Students will demonstrate their understanding of the text on four levels: factual, interpretive, critical and personal.

3. Students will study Twain's use of humor and satire.

4. Students will be given the opportunity to practice reading aloud and silently to improve their skills in each area.

5. Students will answer questions to demonstrate their knowledge and understanding of the main events and characters in *The Adventures of Tom Sawyer* as they relate to the author's theme development.

6. Students will enrich their vocabularies and improve their understanding of the novel through the vocabulary lessons prepared for use in conjunction with the novel.

7. The writing assignments in this unit are geared to several purposes:
   a. To have students demonstrate their abilities to inform, to persuade, or to express their own personal ideas
      Note: Students will demonstrate ability to write effectively to <u>inform</u> by developing and organizing facts to convey information. Students will demonstrate the ability to write effectively to <u>persuade</u> by selecting and organizing relevant information, establishing an argumentative purpose, and by designing an appropriate strategy for an identified audience. Students will demonstrate the ability to write effectively to <u>express personal ideas</u> by selecting a form and its appropriate elements.
   b. To check the students' reading comprehension
   c. To make students think about the ideas presented by the novel
   d. To encourage logical thinking
   e. To provide an opportunity to practice good grammar and improve students' use of the English language.

8. Students will read aloud, report, and participate in large and small group discussions to improve their public speaking and personal interaction skills.

READING ASSIGNMENT SHEET - *The Adventures of Tom Sawyer*

Date Assigned	Chapters Assigned	Completion Date
	1-4	
	5-8	
	9-12	
	13-16	
	17-22	
	23-28	
	29-31	
	32-35	

UNIT OUTLINE - *The Adventures of Tom Sawyer*

1	2	3	4	5
Introduction Project PV 1-4	Project	Read 1 O Read 2-5 S PV 5-8	Read 6-7 O Read 8 S PV 9-12	Read 9 O Read 10-11 S PV 13-16
6 Read 12-13 O Read 14-15 S PV 17-22	**7** Read 16 O Read 17 S Writing Assignment # 1	**8** Read 18-19 O Read 20-24 S PV 23-28	**9** Read 25-26 O Read 27-33 S PV 29-35	**10** Read 33 O Read 34-35 S
11 Writing Assignment #2	**12** Vocabulary	**13** Extra ?s	**14** Extra ?s	**15** Writing Assignment #3 Writing Conf.
16 Nonfiction Reports	**17** Planning Tom Sawyer Day	**18** Planning Tom Sawyer Day	**19** Review	**20** Test
21 Tom Sawyer Day				

Key: P=Preview Study Questions V=Prereading Vocabulary Worksheet O=Orally S=Silently

STUDY GUIDE QUESTIONS

SHORT ANSWER STUDY GUIDE QUESTIONS - *The Adventures of Tom Sawyer*

Chapters 1-4
1. How did Tom get out of being switched?
2. How did Aunt Polly catch Tom for playing hookey?
3. Why does Tom live with his Aunt Polly?
4. What did Tom do to the new boy?
5. What was Tom's Saturday job for punishment? How did he escape doing it? What did he do instead?
6. What was Tom's reward for whitewashing the fence?
7. Why didn't Aunt Polly belt Sid for breaking the sugar bowl?
8. What did a pupil get when he had ten yellow tickets?
9. How did Tom get his ten yellow tickets?
10. How was Tom's deceitfulness revealed?

Chapters 5-8
1. Why did Tom sit next to the aisle in church?
2. Why had Tom enjoyed this Sunday's sermon?
3. Why did Tom sometimes wish that there were no weekend?
4. Why was Tom the center of attention at school the next day?
5. Identify Huck Finn.
6. What are dead cats good for, according to Tom?
7. Next to whom did Tom have to sit, and what did his note to her say?
8. What did Joe and Tom play with during the lessons?
9. What did Tom and Becky do at school during recess?
10. Why did Becky get mad at Tom?
11. What did Tom decide to be?
12. On what did Tom blame the unsuccessful marble spell?

Chapters 9-12
1. Identify Injun Joe, Muff Potter, and Dr. Robinson.
2. Why did Huck and Tom decide to keep mum about the graveyard incident?
3. How did Aunt Polly know that Tom had gone out in the middle of the night?
4. Why did the school master let out school?
5. How did Tom try to keep from talking in his sleep?
6. Why did Tom bring things to Muff Potter in jail?
7. Why did the villagers not tar and feather Injun Joe?
8. What happened to Peter the cat?

The Adventures of Tom Sawyer Short Answer Study Guide Page 2

Chapters 13-16
1. Who joined Tom in his "life of crime"?
2. Why was Huck suddenly disappointed about the state of his clothes?
3. Why couldn't Tom and Joe get to sleep very easily?
4. How do the townspeople find drowned bodies in the river?
5. Why did the boys suddenly feel like heroes?
6. Where did Tom go that night?
7. What were Mrs. Harper and Aunt Polly saying about their boys?
8. What did Huck teach Tom and Joe to do? What happened to them?

Chapters 17-22
1. How did Becky react to Tom's "death"?
2. What was one "poor chap's" claim to fame?
3. Where did the boys hide during the funeral sermon?
4. What did Aunt Polly do to Tom and Huck upon their return?
5. What was Tom's "dream"?
6. What did Tom do to anger Becky? Why?
7. What did Alfred do to Tom's spelling book?
8. Why was Aunt Polly angry with Tom?
9. How did Aunt Polly know Tom was telling the truth about the bark?
10. What made Becky tear the teacher's book?
11. What noble thing did Tom do?
12. How did the boys steal Mr. Dobbins' wig? Why?

Chapters 23-28
1. Who did Muff Potter's attorney call to the stand?
2. What did Tom tell the court?
3. How did the townspeople react to Tom's telling on Injun Joe?
4. Why were Tom's nights scary?
5. Who did Tom invite to go treasure hunting?
6. Why did Tom and Huck go back to the dead limb tree at midnight?
7. Why did the boys stop treasure hunting?
8. Who was the Spaniard?
9. Why were the boys distressed that they had left the spade and pick downstairs?
10. Why did Tom think that maybe the adventure was a dream?
11. What plan did Tom and Huck make for finding the real treasure?
12. How did Tom get in to the Number Two?
13. What scared Tom when he got in to the Number Two?

The Adventures of Tom Sawyer Short Answer Study Guide Page 3

Chapters 29-31
   1. Against whom was the revenge job about which Injun Joe spoke?
   2. Who saved the Widow Douglas?
   3. What ended the search for the two men who were near Widow Douglas' house?
   4. How did Tom and Becky get lost in the cave?
   5. Why did Tom blow out Becky's candle?
   6. Who else was in the cave at the same time as Becky and Tom?

Chapters 32-35
   1. How were Becky and Tom saved?
   2. What happened to Injun Joe?
   3. Where was the real "Number Two"?
   4. How much money was in the treasure?
   5. How much money did Tom get every day?
   6. How did Tom convince Huck to stay with the Widow Douglas?

ANSWER KEY: SHORT ANSWER STUDY GUIDE QUESTIONS
The Adventures of Tom Sawyer

Chapters 1-4

1. How did Tom get out of being switched?
    He told his aunt to look behind her, and when she did, he ran away.

2. How did Aunt Polly catch Tom for playing hookey?
    Sid reminded her that she sewed Tom's shirt collar with white thread and that now it was sewn with black thread. Aunt Polly then knew that Tom had taken his shirt off, gone swimming and then resown it.

3. Why does Tom live with his Aunt Polly?
    He lives with her because his mother, Aunt Polly's sister, died.

4. What did Tom do to the new boy?
    He picked a fight with him and then beat him up.

5. What was Tom's Saturday job for punishment? How did he escape doing it? What did he do instead?
    He was supposed to whitewash the fence, but he got the boys in the neighborhood to do it for him by telling them what fun whitewashing is and how not just everyone can do it. Tom just sat back and watched and collected "trading stuff" the boys gave him to let them whitewash the fence.

6. What was Tom's reward for whitewashing the fence?
    Aunt Polly gave him an apple and a compliment.

7. Why didn't Aunt Polly belt Sid for breaking the sugar bowl?
    She assumed that Tom did it because that is the kind of thing that Tom often does. It never occurred to her that Sid might have done it.

8. What did a pupil get when he had ten yellow tickets?
    The owner of ten yellow tickets was rewarded with a bible.

9. How did Tom get his ten yellow tickets?
    He didn't earn them by memorizing bible verses, he traded stuff with other kids to get his tickets.

10. How was Tom's deceitfulness revealed?
    When asked the names of the first two disciples, Tom replied "David and Goliath." A pupil who had earned ten yellow tickets would have known the correct answer.

Chapters 5-8

1. Why did Tom sit next to the aisle in church?
   He wanted to sit as far away from the window and the tempting sunlight as possible. It was a way to help him pay attention and behave.

2. Why had Tom enjoyed this Sunday's sermon?
   He had passed the time watching a pinch-bug in the aisle, and its conflict with a loose poodle.

3. Why did Tom sometimes wish that there were no weekend?
   After having such a good time on the weekend, going back to school on Monday was exceptionally hard.

4. Why was Tom the center of attention at school the next day?
   He had lost a tooth and could spit through the gap in his remaining teeth.

5. Identify Huck Finn.
   Huck Finn is the son of the town's drunk. He is the envy of all the boys because he can do whatever he pleases with no grownups telling him what to do. He becomes a member of Tom Sawyer's gang.

6. What are dead cats good for, according to Tom?
   They are good for curing warts.

7. Next to whom did Tom have to sit, and what did his note to her say?
   He had to sit next to Becky Thatcher, and his note said, "I love you."

8. What did Joe and Tom play with during the lessons?
   They played with a tick on a slate.

9. What did Tom and Becky do at school during recess?
   They became engaged.

10. Why did Becky get mad at Tom?
    He mentioned that he had been engaged before, to Amy Lawrence.

11. What did Tom decide to be?
    He decided to become a pirate.

12. On what did Tom blame the unsuccessful marble spell?
    He blamed the failure on witches.

Chapters 9-12

1. Identify Injun Joe, Muff Potter, and Dr. Robinson.
    Tom and Huck saw these three men robbing a grave. Injun Joe saw the opportunity to kill Dr. Robinson and did so, blaming the drunken Muff Potter, who couldn't remember enough to say otherwise.

2. Why did Huck and Tom decide to keep mum about the graveyard incident?
    They were both terrified of Injun Joe.

3. How did Aunt Polly know that Tom had gone out in the middle of the night?
    Sid told her. Sid can be a real ratfink underneath his angelic exterior.

4. Why did the school master let out school?
    A "gory knife" was found next to the late Dr. Robinson. This was a major event in the town, and everyone went to investigate it.

5. How did Tom try to keep from talking in his sleep?
    He complained of a toothache and bandaged his jaw shut.

6. Why did Tom bring things to Muff Potter in jail?
    It helped to ease his conscience; he felt guilty for not speaking out to proclaim Muff's innocence.

7. Why did the villagers not tar and feather Injun Joe?
    They were all afraid of him; no one would lead the mob.

8. What happened to Peter the cat?
    Tom gave him some painkiller, making the cat run around the room as if he were crazy.

Chapters 13-16

1. Who joined Tom in his "life of crime"?
    Huck and Joe joined him.

2. Why was Huck suddenly disappointed about the state of his clothes?
    Joe said that pirates wore fancy clothes, and Huck's were shabby.

3. Why couldn't Tom and Joe get to sleep very easily?
    Their consciences were bothering them because they had stolen things.

4. How do the townspeople find drowned bodies in the river?
    They shoot a cannon over the water and float a loaf of bread filled with quicksilver in it on the water. This supposedly makes the body stop and float.

5. Why did the boys suddenly feel like heroes?
   The townspeople thought Huck, Tom and Joe are dead. The boys are the talk of the town, and they were enjoying their notoriety.

6. Where did Tom go that night?
   He sneaked away from the island and went to Aunt Polly's house to see what was going on there.

7. What were Mrs. Harper and Aunt Polly saying about their boys?
   They said that their boys were not really bad, only mischievous and that they would never hit the boys again if only they were alive.

8. What did Huck teach Tom and Joe to do? What happened to them?
   Huck taught them how to smoke and both boys got sick.

Chapters 17-22
1. How did Becky react to Tom's "death"?
   She was depressed and regretful.

2. What was one "poor chap's" claim to fame?
   The "poor chap" (Alfred, probably) claimed that Tom Sawyer licked him once.

3. Where did the boys hide during the funeral sermon?
   They hid in the unused gallery.

4. What did Aunt Polly do to Tom and Huck upon their return?
   Tom got "cuffs and kisses according to Aunt Polly's varying moods," and Huck got hugs because "Somebody's got to be glad to see Huck."

5. What was Tom's "dream"?
   His dream was what he really saw the night he came back to Aunt Polly's house.

6. What did Tom do to anger Becky? Why?
   He flirted with Amy Lawrence. He was jealous because Becky was talking with Alfred.

7. What did Alfred do to Tom's spelling book?
   He spilled ink on it.

8. Why was Aunt Polly angry with Tom?
   She was angry because she found out that Tom's dream was no dream at all, that he had actually returned.

9. How did Aunt Polly know Tom was telling the truth about the bark?
>   She reached into the pocket of his jacket, and the bark was there.

10. What made Becky tear the teacher's book?
>   Tom came in unexpectedly and startled her, causing her to tear the book.

11. What noble thing did Tom do?
>   He took the blame for tearing the teacher's book in order to spare Becky.

12. How did the boys steal Mr. Dobbins' wig? Why?
>   They suspended a cat on a string over Mr. Dobbins' head and lowered the cat until its flailing paws hooked Mr. Dobbins' wig in its claws. They wanted revenge for his being so mean to them.

Chapters 23-28

1. Who did Muff Potter's attorney call to the stand?
>   He called Thomas Sawyer.

2. What did Tom tell the court?
>   He told them that he was a witness that Injun Joe had actually murdered Dr. Robinson.

3. How did the townspeople react to Tom's telling on Injun Joe?
>   They were proud of him and printed his name in the newspaper.

4. Why were Tom's nights scary?
>   He dreamed of Injun Joe.

5. Who did Tom invite to go treasure hunting?
>   He invited Huck Finn to go treasure hunting.

6. Why did Tom and Huck go back to the dead limb tree at midnight?
>   They went back because you have to dig for treasure where the shadow of a dead limb falls at midnight.

7. Why did the boys stop treasure hunting?
>   It was Friday, and bad things happen in haunted houses on Fridays. Also, Huck had a dream about rats, and rats are a sure sign of trouble.

8. Who was the Spaniard?
>   Injun Joe was the Spaniard.

9. Why were the boys distressed that they had left the spade and pick downstairs?
    If the boys had not left the pick and spade downstairs, Injun Joe and his partner would have left the buried treasure right where Huck and Tom could have easily dug it up for themselves.

10. Why did Tom think that maybe the adventure was a dream?
    The amount of money in the treasure was "too vast to be real."

11. What plan did Tom and Huck make for finding the real treasure?
    They would sneak into the alley at night. While Tom would break in to Number Two, Huck would keep watch.

12. How did Tom get in to the Number Two?
    He walked in; the door was unlocked.

13. What scared Tom when he got in to the Number Two?
    He saw Injun Joe there.

Chapters 29-31

1. Against whom was the revenge job about which Injun Joe spoke?
    It was supposed to be against the Widow Douglas.

2. Who saved the Widow Douglas?
    The Welshman did.

3. What ended the search for the two men who were near Widow Douglas' house?
    People discovered that Tom and Becky were missing.

4. How did Tom and Becky get lost in the cave?
    They went "discovering" and lost their way.

5. Why did Tom blow out Becky's candle?
    He knew they needed to conserve candles; there was no use in keeping both of their candles burning at once.

6. Who else was in the cave at the same time as Becky and Tom?
    Injun Joe was.

Chapters 32-35

1. How were Becky and Tom saved?

    Tom went exploring and saw a patch of daylight. He followed the daylight and found a small exit near the Mississippi River. Tom hailed the people on a skiff and they took Becky and Tom towards home.

2. What happened to Injun Joe?

    He got trapped in the cave and died.

3. Where was the real "Number Two"?

    It was in the cave.

4. How much money was in the treasure?

    There was a little over twelve thousand dollars.

5. How much money did Tom get every day?

    He got a dollar every week day and a half a dollar on Sundays.

6. How did Tom convince Huck to stay with the Widow Douglas?

    He told Huck he couldn't be in the gang unless he stayed with the widow and became respectable.

MULTIPLE CHOICE STUDY GUIDE/QUIZ QUESTIONS - *The Adventures of Tom Sawyer*

<u>Chapters 1-4</u>

1. How did Tom get out of being switched?
    A. He sat down on the ground and refused to move.
    B. He cried and begged for mercy until Aunt Polly gave in.
    C. He told his aunt to look behind her, and when she did, he ran away.
    D. He put a pillow inside his pants. He hollered when she hit him, even though it didn't hurt.

2. How did Aunt Polly catch Tom for playing hookey?
    A. She was out picking berries and she saw him through the trees.
    B. Sid reminded her that she sewed Tom's shirt collar with white thread and now it was sewn with black. She knew Tom had taken his shirt off, gone swimming and then resewn it.
    C. She listened to him talking in his sleep and confronted him the next morning.
    D. She asked Sid what the teacher had taught that day. When Tom got home, she asked him to repeat the day's lessons. He tried to bluff his way through, but was not successful. He knew he had been caught.

3. Why does Tom live with his Aunt Polly?
    A. He lives with her because his mother, Aunt Polly's sister, is dead.
    B. He was left on her doorstep as a baby. She didn't think it was right for him to call her "mother," so he calls her "Aunt Polly."
    C. Her oldest brother had too many children to take care of, and Polly needed help around the house. They agreed that she would support Tom and he would work for her.
    D. Tom's parents live far out in the hill country. They wanted Tom to have an education, so they sent him to live with Polly, closer to school.

4. What did Tom do to the new boy?
    A. He made friends and introduced him to the others.
    B. Tom ignored the new boy and got the others to do the same thing.
    C. He took him out in the woods, got him lost, and left him there to find his own way home.
    D. He picked a fight and then beat him up.

5. What was Tom's Saturday job for punishment?
    A. He had to clean the outhouse.
    B. He had to whitewash the fence.
    C. He had to weed the garden.
    D. He had to split logs for firewood.

The Adventures of Tom Sawyer Multiple Choice Study Questions Page 2

6. How did he escape doing his punishment?
    A. He got the other boys to do it by telling them how much fun it was and how not everyone could do it.
    B. He forced Sid to do it by threatening to tell all of the other boys that Sid still sucked his thumb at night.
    C. He pretended to hurt his back. He said he couldn't walk, and Aunt Polly took pity on him.
    D. He paid two of the younger boys a penny each to do it for him.

7. What did he do instead?
    A. He took a nap.
    B. He went fishing.
    C. He collected "trading stuff" from the other boys.
    D. He snuck around to open kitchen windows and stole freshly-baked pies that were cooling there.

8. What was Tom's reward for whitewashing the fence?
    A. Aunt Polly gave him a new pair of shoes.
    B. Aunt Polly gave him an apple and a compliment.
    C. Aunt Polly gave him two pieces of candy.
    D. Aunt Polly gave him a hug and a kiss. He though it was the worst reward he had ever received.

9. Why didn't Aunt Polly belt Sid for breaking the sugar bowl?
    A. She assumed that Tom did it because that is the kind of thing that Tom often does. It never occurred to her that Sid might have done it.
    B. Tom voluntarily took the blame because he didn't think Sid was strong enough to endure a whipping.
    C. She knew Sid had a violent temper and might try and hit her back.
    D. She had just finished visiting with the minister, who had urged her to be more patient with Tom. The minister told her she would get more cooperation from Tom if she treated him more gently. She was following his advice.

The Adventures of Tom Sawyer Multiple Choice Study Questions Page 3

10. What did a pupil get when he had ten yellow tickets?
    A. The owner of the ten yellow tickets was rewarded with a Bible.
    B. The pupil with the ten yellow tickets was exempt from homework for one week.
    C. When a pupil had ten yellow tickets, he or she received a gold medal and was permitted to sit in the first row, first seat in the classroom. This seat was the place of honor reserved for the best student.
    D. The pupil who earned ten yellow tickets received a writing tablet and two pencils.

11. How did Tom get his ten yellow tickets?
    A. He memorized Bible verses.
    B. He stole them from the other students.
    C. He traded stuff with the other students.
    D. He made his own counterfeit tickets. They looked so authentic that no one could tell the difference.

12. How was Tom's deceitfulness revealed?
    A. Some of the other students told on him.
    B. He felt guilty and confessed his crime to his teacher.
    C. He gave a wrong answer when asked the names of the first two disciples.
    D. His teacher found more yellow tickets in his desk and got suspicious. She knew that no one in the class had ever had more than ten yellow tickets at any one time.

The Adventures of Tom Sawyer Multiple Choice Study Questions Page 4

<u>Chapters 5-8</u>

1. True or False: Tom sat next to the aisle in church because it provided a quick escape in case he couldn't sit through the service.
    A. True
    B. False

2. True or False: Tom had enjoyed this Sunday's sermon because he had passed the time watching a pinch-bug.
    A. True
    B. False

3. True or False: Tom sometimes wished there were no weekends because he actually had more fun in school. Aunt Polly made him work all weekend, and she was much stricter than his teacher.
    A. True
    B. False

4. Why was Tom the center of attention at school the next day?
    A. He was wearing a new shirt, which was very unusual for him.
    B. Aunt Polly had shaved hid head because she thought he had lice. The other students made fun of him.
    C. He had lost a tooth and could spit through the gap in his remaining teeth.
    D. He had told everyone he was going to fake having a fit so that he could interrupt the lessons and upset the teacher. They were all waiting eagerly for his performance.

5. Who is Huck Finn?
    A. He is the mayor's step-son. He is rich and buys things for the other boys, so they like him.
    B. He is a new boy in town. He is a bully who has set out to win the allegiance of the other boys away from Tom.
    C. He is the son of the town's drunk. He is the envy of all the boys because he can do whatever he pleases with no grownups telling him what to do.
    D. He is the smartest, most polite boy in the class. Tom has taken it upon himself to "reform" Huck into a more acceptable peer.

The Adventures of Tom Sawyer Multiple Choice Study Questions Page 5

6. What are dead cats good for, according to Tom?
    A. They are good for scaring away witches.
    B. They are good for curing warts.
    C. They bring monetary fortune if they are buried at midnight on the third night after a full moon.
    D. They can be sold to sportsmen who use them to train their hunting dogs.

7. Next to whom did Tom have to sit, and what did the note he sent say?
    A. He had to sit next to Becky Thatcher. His note said, "I love you."
    B. He had to sit next to Huck Finn. His note said, "Let's go fishing after lunch."
    C. He had to sit next to Sid, and his note said, "I'll get even!"
    D. He had to sit next to Ben Rogers. His note said, "Do you have any chewing gum?"

8. What did Joe and Tom play with during the lesson?
    A. They played with a hairball Tom had retrieved from his cat.
    B. They played with a twig and a wad of used chewing gum.
    C. They played with a tick on a slate.
    D. They played with a box of matches.

9. What did Tom and Becky do at school during recess?
    A. They had a mud fight.
    B. They shared their snacks.
    C. Tom let Becky cut his hair.
    D. They became engaged.

10. Why did Becky get mad at Tom?
    A. He told he that going fishing was more important to him than having a girlfriend.
    B. He mentioned that he had been engaged to Amy Lawrence.
    C. She found out that he was not religious, and she was very religious.
    D. He asked her to help him with his homework. She thought he didn't really like her; he only wanted her help.

11. What did Tom decide to be?
    A. He decided to become a pirate.
    B. He decided to become a hermit.
    C. He decided to become a cabin boy on a steamship.
    D. He decided to become a soldier.

The Adventures of Tom Sawyer Multiple Choice Study Questions Page 6

12. On what did Tom blame the unsuccessful marble spell.
    A. He blamed the failure on the full moon.
    B. He blamed the failure on Amy Lawrence.
    C. He blamed the failure on witches.
    D. He blamed the failure on a dead cat.

The Adventures of Tom Sawyer Multiple Choice Study Questions Page 7

Chapters 9 - 12

1. Tom and Huck saw three men robbing a grave. Which of these was not one of the men?
    A. Injun Joe
    B. Dr. Robinson
    C. Bull Harbison
    D. Muff Potter

2. Why did Injun Joe kill the doctor?
    A. It was to settle an old score. Five years earlier, the doctor had insulted Injun Joe and refused to give him food. Injun Joe was still angry.
    B. The doctor was refusing to pay them for their work.
    C. Someone else in town who didn't like the doctor had paid Injun Joe to do it.
    D. Injun Joe got superstitious at the last minute. He didn't want anyone to find out he was involved with digging up the grave, so he decided to kill the witnesses. Unfortunately, he only managed to kill one of them.

3. True or False: Injun Joe blamed Muff Potter for the murder. Muff was so drunk that he didn't remember whether he committed it or not.
    A. True
    B. False

4. Why did Huck and Tom decide to keep mum about the graveyard incident?
    A. They didn't want anyone, especially Aunt Polly, to find out they had been out of bed that night.
    B. They were terrified of Injun Joe.
    C. Neither liked Muff Potter. They thought he got what he deserved, even if he wasn't guilty of the murder.
    D. They were waiting until a reward was offered for information. Then they were going to tell all, get the reward money, and run away.

5. How did Aunt Polly know that Tom had gone out in the middle of the night?
    A. She saw the mud on his shoes.
    B. Sid told on Tom.
    C. She had checked his bed and found it empty.
    D. He was tired the next morning, and couldn't get up for school.

The Adventures of Tom Sawyer Multiple Choice Study Questions Page 8

6. When the "gory knife" was found, the schoolmaster kept the children locked in the schoolhouse to protect them, in case the murderer was still in the area.
    A. True
    B. False

7. How did Tom try to keep from talking in his sleep?
    A. He took elixir before he went to be. He hoped it would knock him out and he would sleep too soundly to talk.
    B. He decided to stay awake all night, so he put rocks under his covers to make the bed too uncomfortable to sleep in.
    C. He complained of a toothache and bandaged his jaw shut.
    D. He slept with a pillow over his head so Sid couldn't hear him.

8. True or False: Tom brought things to Muff Potter in jail to ease his own conscience.
    A. True
    B. False

9. True of False: The villagers didn't tar and feather Injun Joe because they could not prove that he was involved in the murder.
    A. True
    B. False

10. What happened to Peter the cat?
    A. Injun Joe killed him to remind the towns people of his meanness.
    B. Tom put him on Becky Thatcher's doorstep as a present. She didn't want him and had her father take him to the woods and leave him there.
    C. He got in a fight with a dog and was severely injured.
    D. Tom gave him some painkiller, which made the cat act crazy.

The Adventures of Tom Sawyer Multiple Choice Study Questions Page 9

<u>Chapters 13-16</u>

1. True or False: Tom felt driven to pursue his new life of crime because he thought nobody loved him.
    A. True
    B. False

2. Why was Huck suddenly disappointed about the state of his clothes?
    A. He only had one shirt and one pair of pants. He was concerned that he would get cold.
    B. Joe said that pirates wore fancy clothes, and Huck's were shabby.
    C. Tom said that the person with the fewest holes in his pants should be the leader of the gang. Huck had the most holes, so he knew that he could never be the leader.
    D. He was worried that if he stayed away from home too long and outgrew his clothes, he wouldn't get any more.

3. Why couldn't Tom and Joe get to sleep very easily?
    A. They had had a few cups of coffee, and the caffeine was keeping them awake.
    B. The ground was so muddy that they didn't want to lie down. They tried to sleep sitting up, but it was very difficult.
    C. They were afraid of the night noises.
    D. Their consciences were bothering them because they had stolen things.

4. True or False: In order to find drowned bodies in the river, the townspeople shoot a cannon over the water and float a loaf of bread filled with quicksilver in it on the water. This supposedly makes the body stop and float.
    A. True
    B. False

5. True or False: When the boys discover that the townspeople are talking about them because they're supposedly dead, they feel like cowards.
    A. True
    B. False

6. Where did Tom go that night?
    A. He crossed the river to steal food.
    B. He sneaked back to Aunt Polly's house to see what was going on.
    C. He went to visit Becky Thatcher.
    D. He went into town to find a newspaper. He wanted to see if they made the front page.

The Adventures of Tom Sawyer Multiple Choice Study Questions Page 10

7. True or False: Mrs. Harper and Aunt Polly were very angry at the boys. They vowed to beat them if the boys ever showed up again. Mrs. Harper said she would even beat Joe in Heaven, if she met him there.
    A. True
    B. False

8. What did Huck teach Tom and Joe to do?
    A. He taught them how to smoke.
    B. He taught them how to catch fish in their teeth.
    C. He taught them how to walk through the woods without leaving any tracks.
    D. He taught them how to live on roots and berries for food.

9. What was Tom and Joe's reaction to smoking?
    A. They said he was crazy and refused to try it.
    B. They were successful the first time they tried.
    C. Tom liked it but Joe didn't.
    D. They both got sick.

The Adventures of Tom Sawyer Multiple Choice Study Questions Page 11

Chapters 17-22
1. How did Becky react to Tom's "death"?
	A. She was indifferent.
	B. She was relieved.
	C. She was depressed and regretful.
	D. She lost control completely and had to be restrained.

2. What was one "poor chap's" claim to fame?
	A. He had more yellow tickets than any one else in the class.
	B. Tom Sawyer had licked him once.
	C. He had been the last patient treated by Dr. Robinson the night he died.
	D. His parents had given food and clothing to Huck Finn and his father.

3. Where did the boys hide during the funeral sermon?
	A. They hid in the casket.
	B. They hid in back of the altar.
	C. They hid in a tree just outside the church.
	D. They hid in the unused gallery.

4. True or False: When Tom and Huck returned, Aunt Polly beat them both and restricted them to their rooms for a week.
	A. True
	B. False

5. What was Tom's dream?
	A. He dreamed of living with his parents in a big white house.
	B. He dreamed of being buried alive.
	C. He dreamed of marrying Becky Thatcher.
	D. He dreamed of what he really saw the night he came back to Aunt Polly's house.

6. What did Tom do to anger Becky? Why?
	A. He went off with Huck to show her that she wasn't very important to him.
	B. He flirted with Amy Lawrence. He was jealous because Becky was talking with Alfred.
	C. He brought her a bouquet of flowers. She was angry because she knew he had stolen them from someone's garden.
	D. He kissed her in public. She was embarrassed.

The Adventures of Tom Sawyer Multiple Choice Study Questions Page 12

7. What did Alfred do to Tom's spelling book?
	A. He wrote bad words in it.
	B. He tore out a few pages.
	C. He spilled ink on it.
	D. He threw it in the river.

8. Why was Aunt Polly angry with Tom?
	A. She found out that he had actually returned the night he spied on them.
	B. She found out he had rubbed Sid's bedsheets with poison ivy leaves.
	C. She was angry that he liked Becky. She thought he was too young to have a girlfriend.
	D. She told him to give Huck a pair if pants, and he gave Huck his dirtiest, most worn out pair instead of a decent pair.

9. True or False: Aunt Polly found the bark and knew Tom was telling the truth.
	A. True
	B. False

10. What made Becky tear the teacher's book?
	A. It got caught when she pulled the drawer open.
	B. She thought the picture was disgusting. She was trying to tear it out of the book.
	C. She thought there was a spider on the page and she got scared.
	D. She was startled when Tom came in the room.

11. What happened when the teacher asked the students about the book?
	A. Becky admitted what she had done.
	B. The students insisted that Huck Finn had tried to steal the book and got scared off.
	C. Tom took the blame for the incident.
	D. No one would talk, so they all had to write a punishment assignment.

12. What did the boys do on Examination Evening?
	A. They suspended a cat over Mr. Dobbins' head and lowered it until its flailing paws hooked Mr. Dobbins's wig in its claws.
	B. None of them showed up for the school. They had all eaten some wild berries to make themselves sick, and were all home in bed.
	C. They all pretended that they had not learned anything all year.
	D. They stole Mr. Dobbins' book and showed it to their parents.

The Adventures of Tom Sawyer Multiple Choice Study Questions Page 13

Chapters 23-28

1. True or False: Muff's lawyer called Huck Finn to the stand.
    A. True
    B. False

2. True of False: Tom told the court he had witnessed Injun Joe's murder of the doctor.
    A. True
    B. False

3. True or False: The townspeople didn't believe him and ignored his testimony.
    A. True
    B. False

4. Why were Tom's nights scary?
    A. He was always afraid Sid would tell on him for something.
    B. He dreamed of Injun Joe.
    C. Aunt Polly was reading him Bible stories about sinners and their punishment. The stories gave him nightmares.
    D. He started walking in his sleep, and he never knew where he might wake up.

5. Who did Tom invite to go treasure hunting?
    A. He invited Huck Finn.
    B. He invited Aunt Polly.
    C. He invited Becky Thatcher.
    D. He invited Alfred.

6. True or False: Tom and Huck went back to the dead limb tree at midnight because they thought the best time to dig for treasure was where the shadow of a dead limb falls at midnight.
    A. True
    B. False

7. Why did the boys stop treasure hunting?
    A. They were hungry and went home to eat.
    B. It was dark and they didn't have any means of lighting their way.
    C. It was Friday and bad things happen in haunted houses on Fridays.
    D. They got tired of digging and went fishing instead.

The Adventures of Tom Sawyer Multiple Choice Study Questions Page 14

8. What did they find out about the Spaniard?
    A. He was the previous owner of the old house, who came back in disguise to claim the treasure.
    B. He was really Injun Joe.
    C. He was a renegade from the Mexican army.
    D. He could also speak English and French.

9. True or False: The boys were distressed that they had left the spade and pick downstairs. If they had not done so, then Injun Joe and his partner would have left the treasure right where Huck and Tom could easily have dug it up for themselves.
    A. True
    B. False

10. True or False: Tom thought the adventure was a dream because he had never worked so hard before. He couldn't imagine really working that hard, even to dig up a treasure.
    A. True
    B. False

11. What plan did Tom and Huck make for finding the real treasure?
    A. They would sneak into the alley at night. While Huck would break in to Number Two, Tom would keep each.
    B. They would sneak into the alley at night. While Tom would break in to Number Two, Huck would keep watch.
    C. They would let Joe in on their plans. Joe and Huck would keep watch while Tom broke in and took the money.
    D. They would masquerade as cleaning boys. They would go into the room in broad daylight, while the occupants were out and take the treasure.

12. How did the burglar(s) get in to the Number Two?
    A. Through the unlocked door
    B. By breaking the window and climbing in
    C. By stealing the key from the clerk
    D. By paying the tavern keeper to open the room

13. What scared the burglar(s) when he/they got into Number Two?
    A. There was a noose hanging from the ceiling.
    B. There were guns and knives all over the room.
    C. The bed was covered with blood.
    D. Injun Joe was there.

The Adventures of Tom Sawyer Multiple Choice Study Questions Page 15

<u>Chapters 29-31</u>
1. Against whom was the revenge job which Injun Joe spoke?
    A. It was against Judge Thatcher.
    B. It was against Aunt Polly
    C. It was against the Widow Douglas.
    D. It was against Dr. Robinson's family.

2. Who saved the victim of the revenge plot?
    A. Tom did.
    B. The Welshman did.
    C. The Widow Douglas did.
    D. The town sheriff did.

3. What ended the search for the two men near the victim's house?
    A. People discovered that Tom and Becky were missing.
    B. The victim had a heart attack and had to be rushed to the doctor.
    C. The men were captured.
    D. A fierce thunder and lightning storm started. The search had to be called off.

4. What were Tom and Becky doing?
    A. They went for a walk, got tired, and took shelter in an old barn, where they fell asleep.
    B. Tom convinced Becky to go rafting with him and they took off down the river.
    C. Tom wanted to show Becky his clubhouse on the island.
    D. They went exploring in the cave and lost their way.

5. Why did Tom blow out Becky's candle?
    A. He wanted to try and get romantic.
    B. He was superstitious about burning a candle that was shorter than five inches. He thought it was bad luck.
    C. He knew they needed to conserve candles.
    D. He thought he had extra-sensitive eyes that could see better in the dark.

6. Who else was in the same location at the same time as Becky and Tom?
    A. Muff Potter was.
    B. Huck Finn's father was.
    C. Mr. Thatcher was.
    D. Injun Joe was.

The Adventures of Tom Sawyer Multiple Choice Study Questions Page 16

Chapters 32- 35
1. True or False: Tom saved them by finding an exit near the Mississippi River. He hailed some people on a skiff and they took Tom and Becky home.
    A. True
    B. False

2. What happened to Injun Joe?
    A. He escaped and was never seen again.
    B. He was arrested and sent to jail.
    C. He got trapped in the cave and died.
    D. No one was ever sure. He just disappeared.

3. Where was the real "Number Two"?
    A. It was in the hotel.
    B. It was on the second floor of the old house.
    C. It was in the cave.
    D. It was the second island in the river, just south of the town.

4. How much money was in the treasure?
    A. There was a little over twelve thousand dollars.
    B. There was a half-million dollars.
    C. There was only seventy five dollars.
    D. There was fifty thousand dollars.

5. What happened to the money?
    A. They had to give it all to the owners of the old house.
    B. They buried it in two separate places so no one would find it. They planned to spend it when they were older.
    C. Judge Thatcher and the Widow Douglas invested the money for the boys.
    D. Aunt Polly put Tom's in the bank. Huck's father heard the news, and came back to town to claim all of Huck's money. He then wasted it on liquor.

6. True or False: Tom convinced Huck to stay with the Widow Douglas by playing on Huck's sympathy. Tom said the Widow was too old and fragile to be left alone, and a good, strong boy like Huck owed it to her to help out.
    A. True
    B. False

ANSWER KEY - MULTIPLE CHOICE STUDY/QUIZ QUESTIONS
The Adventures of Tom Sawyer

	Chapters 1 - 4	Chapters 5 - 8	Chapters 9 - 12	Chapters 13 - 16	Chapters 17 - 22	Chapters 23 - 28	Chapters 29 - 31	Chapters 32 - 35
1.	C	B	C	A	C	B	C	A
2.	B	A	A	B	B	A	B	C
3.	A	B	A	D	D	B	A	C
4.	D	C	B	A	B	B	D	A
5.	B	C	B	B	D	A	C	C
6.	A	B	B	B	B	A	D	B
7.	C	A	C	B	C	C		
8.	B	C	A	A	A	B		
9.	A	D	B	D	A	A		
10.	A	B	D		D	B		
11.	C	A			C	B		
12.	C	C			A	A		
13.						D		

PREREADING VOCABULARY WORKSHEETS

Vocabulary - *The Adventures of Tom Sawyer*

<u>Chapters 1 - 4</u> Part I: Using Prior Knowledge and Contextual Clues

Below are the sentences in which the vocabulary words appear in the text. Read the sentence. Use any clues you can find in the sentence combined with your prior knowledge, and write what you think the underlined words mean on the lines provided.

1. She looked <u>perplexed</u> for a moment, and then said . . . .

_____

2. The new boy took two broad coppers out of his pocket and held them out with <u>derision</u>.

_____

3. Tom considered, was about to <u>consent</u>; but he altered his mind.

_____

4. Tom gave up the brush with reluctance in his face, but <u>alacrity</u> in his heart.

_____

5. . . . in order to make a man or a boy <u>covet</u> a thing, it is only necessary to make the thing difficult to attain.

_____

6. These two great commanders did not <u>condescend</u> to fight in person .... but . . . . conducted the field operations by orders delivered through aides-de-camp.

_____

7. Tom <u>contrived</u> to scarify the cupboard with it, and was arranging to begin . . . when he was called off to dress for Sunday school.

_____

8. The middle-aged man turned out to be a <u>prodigious</u> personage--no less than the county judge--

_____

Vocabulary - *The Adventures of Tom Sawyer* Chapters 1-4 Continued

Part II: Determining the Meaning: Match the vocabulary words to their dictionary definitions.

___ 1. perplexed   A. eagerness
___ 2. derision   B. lower oneself to the position of inferiors
___ 3. consent   C. schemed
___ 4. alacrity   D. puzzled, uncertain
___ 5. covet   E. impressively great
___ 6. condescend   F. ridicule
___ 7. contrived   G. agree to something
___ 8. prodigious   H. want

Vocabulary - *The Adventures of Tom Sawyer* Chapters 5 - 8

Part I: Using Prior Knowledge and Contextual Clues
Below are the sentences in which the vocabulary words appear in the text. Read the sentence. Use any clues you can find in the sentence combined with your prior knowledge, and write what you think the underlined words mean on the lines provided.

9. . . . closed with the <u>supplication</u> that the words he was about to speak might find grace and favor, and be as seed sown in fertile ground, yielding in time a grateful harvest of good.

_____

10. So he went to the beetle and began a <u>wary</u> attack on it again . . . .

_____

11. He generally began that day with wishing he had had no intervening holiday, it made the going into captivity and fetters again so much more <u>odious</u>.

_____

12. The groans <u>ceased</u> and the pain vanished from the toe.

_____

13. His heart was heavy, and he said with a <u>disdain</u> which he did not feel, the it wasn't anything to spit like Tom Sawyer . . . .

_____

14. Tom partly uncovered a dismal <u>caricature</u> of a house with two gable ends to it and a corkscrew of smoke issuing from the chimney.

_____

15. Tom was swimming in <u>bliss</u>.

_____

16. So she sat down to cry again and <u>upbraid</u> herself. . . .

_____

17. No--better still, he would . . . <u>sear</u> the eyeballs of all his companions with unappeasable envy.

_____

Tom Sawyer Vocabulary Chapters 5-8 Continued

Part II: Determining the Meaning: Match the vocabulary words to their dictionary definitions.

___ 9. supplication A. stopped
___ 10. wary B. arousing a strong dislike or displeasure
___ 11. odious C. cautious
___ 12. ceased D. burn; scorch
___ 13. disdain E. extreme happiness
___ 14. caricature F. reprimand
___ 15. bliss G. contempt
___ 16. upbraid H. drawing in which the subject's distinctive traits are exaggerated
___ 17. sear I. plea

Vocabulary - *The Adventures of Tom Sawyer* Chapters 9-12

Part I: Using Prior Knowledge and Contextual Clues
   Below are the sentences in which the vocabulary words appear in the text. Read the sentence. Use any clues you can find in the sentence combined with your prior knowledge, and write what you think the underlined words mean on the lines provided.

18. The boys talked little, and only under their breath, for the time and the place and the pervading solemnity and silence oppressed their spirits.

_____

19. Tom's reflections grew oppressive.

_____

20. The moon drifted from behind the clouds and exposed the pallid face.

_____

21. They glanced backward over their shoulders from time to time, apprehensively, as if they feared they might be followed.

_____

22. Then they separated, cogitating.

_____

23. It seemed to Tom that his schoolmates never would get done holding inquests on dead cats, and thus keeping his trouble present to his mind.

_____

24. Then he went tearing around the house again spreading chaos and destruction in his path.

_____

Part II: Determining the Meaning: Match the vocabulary words to their dictionary definitions.

___ 18. pervading   A. judicial inquiry into the cause of a death
___ 19. oppressive   B. disorder; confusion
___ 20. pallid   C. anxiously
___ 21. apprehensively   D. pale, dull, lifeless
___ 22. cogitating   E. thinking
___ 23. inquests   F. present throughout
___ 24. chaos   G. difficult to bear

Vocabulary - *The Adventures of Tom Sawyer* Chapters 13 - 16

Part I: Using Prior Knowledge and Contextual Clues

Below are the sentences in which the vocabulary words appear in the text. Read the sentence. Use any clues you can find in the sentence combined with your prior knowledge, and write what you think the underlined words mean on the lines provided.

25. . . . wishing "she" could see him now, abroad on the wild sea, facing peril and death with dauntless heart, going to his doom with a grim smile on his lips.

_____

26. The other pirates envied him this majestic vice, and secretly resolved to acquire it shortly.

_____

27. They tried to argue it away by reminding conscience that they had purloined sweetmeats and apples scores of times, but conscience was not to be appeased by such thin plausibilities . . . .

_____

28. Then with a mutual impulse the two bereaved women flung themselves into each other's arms and had a good, consoling cry, and then parted.

_____

29. They were a vain and boastful company of heroes when the tale was done.

_____

30. . . . splashed water in each other's faces with their palms, gradually approaching each other, with averted faces to avoid the strangling sprays . . . .

_____

31. He had made a plausible excuse; but his real reason had been the fear that not even the secret would keep them with him any very great length of time. . . .

_____

32. The storm culminated in one catchless effort that seemed likely to tear the island to pieces, burn it up, drown it to the treetops, blow it away, and deafen every creature in it, all at one and the same moment.
. . . They boys went back to camp, a good deal awed . . . .

_____

Tom Sawyer Vocabulary Chapters 13-16 Continued

Part II: Determining the Meaning - Match the vocabulary words to their dictionary definitions.

___ 25. dauntless
___ 26. vice
___ 27. appeased
___ 28. mutual
___ 29. vain
___ 30. averted
___ 31. plausible
___ 32. awed

A. possessed in common
B. excessively proud
C. believable
D. fearless
E. bad habit
F. amazed with mixed emotions of reverence, respect and dread
G. calmed; satisfied; pacified
H. turned away

Vocabulary - *The Adventures of Tom Sawyer* Chapters 17 - 22

Part I: Using Prior Knowledge and Contextual Clues
Below are the sentences in which the vocabulary words appear in the text. Read the sentence. Use any clues you can find in the sentence combined with your prior knowledge, and write what you think the underlined words mean on the lines provided.

33. In the afternoon Becky Thatcher found herself moping about the deserted schoolhouse yard, and feeling very melancholy.

_____

34. Aunt Polly, Mary, and the Harpers threw themselves upon their restored ones, smothered them with kisses and poured out thanksgivings, while poor Huck stood abashed and uncomfortable, not knowing what to do or where to hide from so many unwelcoming eyes.

_____

35. He did not hear what Amy was saying, and whenever she paused expectantly he could only stammer an awkward assent, which was as often misplaced as otherwise.

_____

36. His smartness of the morning had seemed to Tom a good joke before, and very ingenious.

_____

37. As the great day approached, all the tyranny that was in him came to the surface; he seemed to take a vindictive pleasure in punishing the least shortcomings.

_____

38. Homely truth is unpalatable.

_____

39. He promised to abstain from smoking, chewing, and profanity as long as he remained a member.

_____

Part II: Determining the Meaning: Match the vocabulary words to their dictionary definitions.

___ 33. melancholy   A. ruler's unjust use of power
___ 34. abashed   B. stop doing something by one's own choice
___ 35. assent   C. clever; inventive
___ 36. ingenious   D. agreement
___ 37. tyranny   E. depressed; sad; gloomy
___ 38. unpalatable   F. ashamed; uneasy; disconcerted
___ 39. abstain   G. unacceptable to the mind or senses

Vocabulary - *The Adventures of Tom Sawyer* Chapters 23 - 28

Part I: Using Prior Knowledge and Contextual Clues
   Below are the sentences in which the vocabulary words appear in the text. Read the sentence. Use any clues you can find in the sentence combined with your prior knowledge, and write what you think the underlined words mean on the lines provided.

40. His gratitude for their gifts had always smote their consciences before--it cut deeper than ever this time.

_____

41. Tom kept his ears open when idlers sauntered out of the courtroom, but invariably heard distressing news--the toils were closing more and more relentlessly around poor Potter.

_____

42. The boys were subdued by these solemnities and talked little.

_____

43. . . . the intolerable distress of the situation woke the stricken resolution of the lads--they were about to spring for the closet, when there was a crash . . . .

_____

44. But the incidents of his adventure grew sensibly sharper and clearer under the attrition of thinking them over . . . .

_____

Part II: Determining the Meaning: Match the vocabulary words to their dictionary definitions.

___ 40. smote   A. determination
___ 41. invariably   B. a gradual rubbing away or wearing down
___ 42. subdued   C. always; without change
___ 43. resolution   D. inflicted a heavy blow upon
___ 44. attrition   E. conquered and brought under control

Vocabulary - *The Adventures of Tom Sawyer* Chapters 29 - 31

Part I: Using Prior Knowledge and Contextual Clues
Below are the sentences in which the vocabulary words appear in the text. Read the sentence. Use any clues you can find in the sentence combined with your prior knowledge, and write what you think the underlined words mean on the lines provided.

45. . . . planted his foot carefully and firmly, after balancing, one-legged, in a precarious way and almost toppling over, first on one side and then on the other.

_____

46. Whispers passed along and a boding uneasiness took possession of every countenance.

_____

47. All the tedious night the town waited for news . . . .

_____

48. . . . and mottoes with which the rock walls had been frescoed (in candle smoke).

_____

49. . . . a little stream of water, trickling over a ledge and carrying a limestone sediment with it, had, in the slow-dragging ages, formed a laced and ruffled Niagara in gleaming and imperishable stone.

_____

50. The poor morsel of food only whetted desire.

_____

Part II: Determining the Meaning: Match the vocabulary words to their dictionary definitions.

___ 45. precarious   A. indestructible
___ 46. countenance   B. painted
___ 47. tedious   C. stimulated; sharpened
___ 48. frescoed   D. face
___ 49. imperishable   E. dangerously lacking in security or stability
___ 50. whetted   F. tiresome by reason of extreme length or slowness

Vocabulary - *The Adventures of Tom Sawyer* Chapters 32 - 35

Part I: Using Prior Knowledge and Contextual Clues

Below are the sentences in which the vocabulary words appear in the text. Read the sentence. Use any clues you can find in the sentence combined with your prior knowledge, and write what you think the underlined words mean on the lines provided.

51,52. The petition had been largely signed; many tearful and eloquent meetings had been held, and a committee of sappy women had been appointed to go in deep mourning and wail around the governor, and implore him to be a merciful ass and trample his duty underfoot.

_____

_____

53. If he had been Satan himself there would have been plenty of weaklings ready to scribble their names to a pardon petition and drip a tear on it from their permanently impaired and leaking waterworks.

_____

54. The candles revealed the fact that it was not really a precipice, but only a steep clay hill twenty or thirty feet high.

_____

55. They presently emerged into the clump of sumac bushes, looked warily out, found the coast clear, and were soon lunching and smoking in the skiff.

_____

56. . . . when she pleaded grace for the mighty lie which Tom had told in order to shift that whipping from her shoulders to his own, the judge said with a fine outburst that it was a noble, a generous, a magnanimous lie--a lie that was worthy to hold up its head and march down through history breast to breast with George Washington's lauded Truth about the hatchet!

_____

Part II: Determining the Meaning: Match the vocabulary words to their dictionary definitions.

___ 51. eloquent   A. damaged; diminished in strength
___ 52. implore   B. cautiously
___ 53. impaired   C. characterized by persuasive, powerful or moving discourse
___ 54. precipice   D. courageously noble
___ 55. warily   E. beg
___ 56. magnanimous   F. overhanging rock; cliff

ANSWER KEY - VOCABULARY
The Adventures of Tom Sawyer

Chapters 1 - 4	Chapters 5 - 8	Chapters 9 - 12
1. D	9. I	18. F
2. F	10. C	19. G
3. G	11. B	20. D
4. A	12. A	21. C
5. H	13. G	22. E
6. B	14. H	23. A
7. C	15. E	24. B
8. E	16. F	
	17. D	

Chapters 13 - 16	Chapters 17 - 22	Chapters 23 - 28
25. D	33. E	40. D
26. E	34. F	41. C
27. G	35. D	42. E
28. A	36. C	43. A
29. B	37. A	44. B
30. H	39. G	
31. C	39. B	
32. F		

Chapters 29 - 31	Chapters 32 - 35
45. E	51. C
46. D	52. E
47. F	53. A
48. B	54. F
49. A	55. B
50. C	56. D

DAILY LESSONS

LESSONS ONE AND TWO

<u>Objectives</u>
    1. To introduce the *Adventures of Tom Sawyer* unit.
    2. To distribute books and other related materials
    3. To preview the study questions for chapters 1-4
    4. To familiarize students with the vocabulary for chapters 1-4
    5. To make the reading project assignment

TEACHER'S NOTE:
    There are several memorable scenes from *Tom Sawyer*. We thought it would be fun for students to dress up in costumes and act out these scenes as you come to them in the reading of the book. It will add interest to the reading, give students a chance to practice public speaking, and add some humor and fun to the unit.
    The reading assignments are divided into sections of about thirty pages, and we've decided to leave them that way on the assignment sheet, study guides and prereading vocabulary worksheets in case you choose not to act out scenes from the novel. However, in the daily lessons, we have refigured the way in which the assignments are read to accommodate the oral presentations of the scenes.

<u>Activity #1</u>
    Distribute the materials students will use in this unit. Explain in detail how students are to use these materials.

    <u>Study Guides</u> Students should read the study guide questions for each reading assignment prior to beginning the reading assignment to get a feeling for what events and ideas are important in the section they are about to read. After reading the section, students will (as a class or individually) answer the questions to review the important events and ideas from that section of the book. Students should keep the study guides as study materials for the unit test.

    <u>Vocabulary</u> Prior to reading a reading assignment, students will do vocabulary work related to the section of the book they are about to read. Following the completion of the reading of the book, there will be a vocabulary review of all the words used in the vocabulary assignments. Students should keep their vocabulary work as study materials for the unit test.

    <u>Reading Assignment Sheet</u> You need to fill in the reading assignment sheet to let students know by when their reading has to be completed. You can either write the assignment sheet up on a side blackboard or bulletin board and leave it there for students to see each day, or you can "ditto" copies for each student to have. In either case, you should advise students to become very familiar with the reading assignments so they know what is expected of them.

<u>Extra Activities Center</u> The Unit Resources section of this unit contains suggestions for an extra library of related books and articles in your classroom as well as crossword and word search puzzles. Make an extra activities center in your room where you will keep these materials for students to use. (Bring the books and articles in from the library and keep several copies of the puzzles on hand.) Explain to students that these materials are available for students to use when they finish reading assignments or other class work early.

<u>Nonfiction Assignment Sheet</u> Explain to students that they each are to read at least one non-fiction piece from the in-class library at some time during the unit. Students will fill out a nonfiction assignment sheet after completing the reading to help you evaluate their reading experiences and to help the students think about and evaluate their own reading experiences.

<u>Books</u> Each school has its own rules and regulations regarding student use of school books. Advise students of the procedures that are normal for your school.

<u>Activity #2</u>

Show students how to preview the study questions and do the prereading vocabulary worksheets for Chapters 1-4 of *The Adventures of Tom Sawyer*. Give students about fifteen minutes to complete this activity.

<u>Activity #3</u>

Distribute the project assignment sheets. Discuss the directions in detail and make the part assignments. Students should use the remainder of the class time in Lesson One and all of the class time in Lesson Two to work with their partner(s) practicing their lines, planning their costumes and deciding where they are going to get their props if they need them.

PART ASSIGNMENTS FOR THE READING PROJECT - *Tom Sawyer*

SCENE TITLE	DUE DATE	CHARACTERS	ASSIGNED TO
Tom and the New Boy		Tom Alfred	
Tom is Dying		Tom Sid Aunt Polly	
Dead Cat		Tom Huck	
I Love You		Tom Becky	
The Engagement		Tom Becky	
Graveyard Murder		Tom Huck Injun Joe Muff Potter Dr Robinson	
The Painkiller and the Cat		Tom Cat Aunt Polly	
Island Boys		Tom Huck Joe	
Island Chatter		Tom Huck Joe	
The Dream		Aunt Polly Tom Mary Sid	
I Didn't Think		Aunt Polly Tom	
Buried Treasure		Tom Huck	
The Haunted House		Tom Huck Injun Joe T'other	
Say It Again, Tom		Tom Huck	

You and a partner (or partners) are going to be assigned a scene from the book. On an appointed day during the reading of the novel, you and your partner(s) will present your scene to the class in full costume, with any necessary props, and to the very best of your acting abilities. This is no time to be shy or bashful; jump right in with both feet and be a real ham.

SCENE TITLE	CH #	FROM	TO	PEOPLE
TOM AND THE NEW BOY	1	The summer evenings were long	the enemy only made faces at him through the window	Tom Alfred
TOM IS DYING	6	Tom lay thinking	The tooth hung dangling from the bedpost	Tom, Sid Aunt Polly
DEAD CAT	6	Hello, Huckleberry!	each feeling wealthier than before	Tom Huck
I LOVE YOU	6	The titter that rippled around the room	but reddened and looked pleased, nevertheless	Tom Becky
THE ENGAGEMENT	7	In a little while the two met at the bottom ...	The end of chapter 7	Tom Becky
GRAVEYARD MURDER	9	Then they waited in silence	The end of chapter 9	Tom, Huck, Inj. Joe, Muff, Dr. R
THE PAINKILLER AND THE CAT	12	One day Tom was in the act of dosing the crack	you needn't take any more medicine	Tom, Cat Aunt Polly
ISLAND BOYS	13	When the last crisp slice of bacon was gone	pirates to start with a proper wardrobe	Tom, Huck Joe
ISLAND CHATTER	16	I bet there's been pirates on this island before	So Huck sat down again	Tom, Huck Joe
THE DREAM	18	Well, I don't say it wasn't a fine joke	go 'long, Sid, Mary, Tom	Aunt Polly, Tom Mary, Sid
I DIDN'T THINK	19	Beginning of chapter 19	End of chapter 19	Aunt Polly, Tom
BURIED TREASURE	25	Beginning of chapter 25	End of chapter 25	Tom, Huck
THE HAUNTED HOUSE	26	Sh!	End of chapter 26	Tom, Huck, Inj. Joe, T'other
SAY IT AGAIN, TOM	33	The morning after the funeral	I won't be gone a minute	Tom, Huck

NONFICTION ASSIGNMENT SHEET
(To be completed after reading the required nonfiction article)

Name _____ Date _____

Title of Nonfiction Read _____

Written By _____ Publication Date _____

I. Factual Summary: Write a short summary of the piece you read.

II. Vocabulary
    1. With which vocabulary words in the piece did you encounter some degree of difficulty?

    2. How did you resolve your lack of understanding with these words?

III. Interpretation: What was the main point the author wanted you to get from reading his work?

IV. Criticism
    1. With which points of the piece did you agree or find easy to accept? Why?

    2. With which points of the piece did you disagree or find difficult to believe? Why?

V. Personal Response: What do you think about this piece? OR How does this piece influence your ideas?

LESSON THREE

Objectives
1. To read chapter 1 orally
2. To give students practice reading orally
3. To evaluate students' oral reading
4. To read chapters 2-5

NOTE: With most of the oral reading assignments, a narrator will be helpful to fill in the lines prior to and/or after the scene being acted. One person could be assigned this job, or you could call on various students to read these parts.

Activity #1
Have students read chapter 1 of *The Adventures of Tom Sawyer* out loud in class. Have a narrator or various students read the parts leading up to the acted scene. Students participating in the acted scene should be set up prior to the time that the reading begins so they can just proceed with their acting and the flow of the story is not interrupted. After the scene is completed, the narrator(s) should continue reading the rest of chapter 1 orally. An evaluation form for the acting of the scenes is included for your convenience.

Activity #2
Tell students that prior to your next class meeting they need to have read chapters 2-5 and to have completed the prereading work (previewing the study questions and doing the prereading vocabulary worksheet) for chapters 5-8. Give students any remaining class time to work on this assignment.

ORAL READING EVALUATION - *Tom Sawyer*

Name _____ Class____ Date _____

SKILL	EXCELLENT	GOOD	AVERAGE	FAIR	POOR
Fluency	5	4	3	2	1
Clarity	5	4	3	2	1
Audibility	5	4	3	2	1
Pronunciation	5	4	3	2	1
Costume	5	4	3	2	1
Acting	5	4	3	2	1
_____	5	4	3	2	1
_____	5	4	3	2	1

Total _____   Grade _____

Comments:

LESSON FOUR

Objectives
1. To review the main events and ideas from chapters 1-4
2. To preview the study questions for chapters 9-12
3. To familiarize students with the vocabulary in chapters 9-12
4. To read chapters 6 and 7 orally
5. To read chapter 8

Activity #1

Give students a few minutes to formulate answers for the study guide questions for chapters 1-4, and then discuss the answers to the questions in detail. Write the answers on the board or overhead transparency so students can have the correct answers for study purposes. Note: It is a good practice in public speaking and leadership skills for individual students to take charge of leading the discussions of the study questions. Perhaps a different student could go to the front of the class and lead the discussion each day that the study questions are discussed during this unit. Of course, the teacher should guide the discussion when appropriate and be sure to fill in any gaps the students leave.

Activity #2

Have students read chapters 6-7 of *The Adventures of Tom Sawyer* out loud in class. Have a narrator or various students read the parts leading up to the acted scene. Students participating in the acted scene should be set up prior to the time that the reading begins so they can just proceed with their acting and the flow of the story is not interrupted. After the scene is completed, the narrator(s) should continue reading the rest of chapters 6-7 orally. An evaluation form for the acting of the scenes is included for your convenience.

Activity #3

Tell students that prior to your next class meeting they need to have read chapter 8 and to have completed the prereading work (previewing the study questions and doing the prereading vocabulary worksheet) for chapters 9-12. Give students any remaining class time to work on this assignment.

LESSON FIVE

Objectives
1. To review the main events and ideas from chapters 5-8
2. To preview the study questions and the vocabulary for chapters 13-16
4. To read chapter 9 orally
5. To read chapters 10-11

Activity #1
    Give students a few minutes to formulate answers for the study guide questions for chapters 5-8, and then discuss the answers to the questions in detail. Write the answers on the board or overhead transparency so students can have the correct answers for study purposes.

Activity #2
    Have students read chapter 9 of *The Adventures of Tom Sawyer* out loud in class. Have a narrator or various students read the parts leading up to the acted scene. Students participating in the acted scene should be set up prior to the time that the reading begins so they can just proceed with their acting and the flow of the story is not interrupted.

Activity #3
    Tell students that prior to your next class meeting they need to have read chapters 10-11 and to have completed the prereading work (previewing the study questions and doing the prereading vocabulary worksheet) for chapters 13-16. Give students any remaining class time to work on this assignment.

LESSON SIX

Objectives
    1. To review the main events and ideas from chapters 9-12
    2. To preview the study questions and the vocabulary for chapters 17-22
    4. To read chapters 12-13 orally
    5. To read chapters 14-15

Activity #1

    Have students read chapters 12 and 13 of *The Adventures of Tom Sawyer* out loud in class. Have a narrator or various students read the parts leading up to the acted scene. Students participating in the acted scene should be set up prior to the time that the reading begins so they can just proceed with their acting and the flow of the story is not interrupted. The narrator(s) should complete reading the chapters after the acted scenes are completed.

Activity #2

    Give students a few minutes to formulate answers for the study guide questions for chapters 9-12, and then discuss the answers to the questions in detail. Write the answers on the board or overhead transparency so students can have the correct answers for study purposes.

Activity #3

    Tell students that prior to your next class meeting they need to have read chapters 14-15 and to have completed the prereading work (previewing the study questions and doing the prereading vocabulary worksheet) for chapters 17-22. Give students any remaining class time to work on this assignment.

LESSON SEVEN

Objectives
1. To read chapter 16 orally
2. To read chapter 17 silently
3. To give students the opportunity to practice writing to express their own ideas
4. To give the teacher the opportunity to evaluate students' writing skills

Activity #1

Have students read chapter 16 of *The Adventures of Tom Sawyer* out loud in class. Have a narrator or various students read the parts leading up to the acted scene. Students participating in the acted scene should be set up prior to the time that the reading begins so they can just proceed with their acting and the flow of the story is not interrupted. The narrator(s) should complete reading the chapters after the acted scenes are completed.

Activity #2

Distribute Writing Assignment #1. Discuss the directions in detail and give students ample time to complete the assignment.

Activity #3

Tell students that prior to your next class period they should have read chapter 17 of *The Adventures of Tom Sawyer*. If they have time after completing the writing assignment, they may begin this reading assignment.

LESSON EIGHT

Objectives
1. To review the main events and ideas from chapters 13-16
2. To preview the study questions and the vocabulary for chapters 23-28
4. To read chapters 18-19 orally
5. To read chapters 20-24

Activity #1
   Give students a few minutes to formulate answers for the study guide questions for chapters 13-16, and then discuss the answers to the questions in detail. Write the answers on the board or overhead transparency so students can have the correct answers for study purposes.

Activity #2
   Have students read chapters 18 and 19 of *The Adventures of Tom Sawyer* out loud in class. Have a narrator or various students read the parts leading up to and after the acted scenes. Students participating in the acted scene should be set up prior to the time that the reading begins so they can just proceed with their acting and the flow of the story is not interrupted.

Activity #3
   Tell students that prior to your next class meeting they need to have read chapters 20-24 and to have completed the prereading work (previewing the study questions and doing the prereading vocabulary worksheet) for chapters 23-28. Give students any remaining class time to work on this assignment.

WRITING ASSIGNMENT #1 - *The Adventures of Tom Sawyer*

PROMPT

The Adventures of Tom Sawyer was written about a period of time prior to the Civil War and prior to the time the industrial revolution had reached the midwest. Through Tom Sawyer and Huck Finn we look back at those times with nostalgia, with the feeling that those days were somehow more simple or better than ours are now. On the other hand, one could consider the lack of modern conveniences and the rougher life people had settling the west.

If I had a time machine and could transport you (and anyone you wanted to take with you) back in time, would you go back to 1840 or would you want to stay here and now? Why? Your assignment is to write a composition in which you answer those questions.

PREWRITING

On a scratch sheet of paper, draw a line down the middle of the page. On the left-hand column write "1840." On the right-hand column write "today." Under each column, write down the advantages of each era.

On another scratch sheet of paper, draw the same set-up as before, only this time write down the disadvantages of each era.

After carefully considering each page of notes, make your decision as to whether or not you would go back in time to 1840 to live.

What three things most led you to your decision? Jot them down.

DRAFTING

Write one paragraph in which you introduce the idea that you would/wouldn't go back in time to 1840 to live.

In the body of your composition, write one paragraph for each of the reasons why you would/wouldn't go back in time. Fill out each paragraph with examples and/or explanations of your reason.

Write a concluding paragraph in which you bring your composition to a close and make your final comments.

PROMPT

When you finish the rough draft of your paper, ask a student who sits near you to read it. After reading your rough draft, he/she should tell you what he/she liked best about your work, which parts were difficult to understand, and ways in which your work could be improved. Reread your paper considering your critic's comments, and make the corrections you think are necessary.

PROOFREADING

Do a final proofreading of your paper double-checking your grammar, spelling, organization, and the clarity of your ideas.

LESSON NINE

Objectives
1. To review the main events and ideas from chapters 17-22
2. To preview the study questions and the vocabulary for chapters 29-35
4. To read chapters 25-26 orally
5. To read chapters 27-33

Activity #1

Give students a few minutes to formulate answers for the study guide questions for chapters 17-22, and then discuss the answers to the questions in detail. Write the answers on the board or overhead transparency so students can have the correct answers for study purposes.

Activity #2

Have students read chapters 25 and 26 of *The Adventures of Tom Sawyer* out loud in class. Have a narrator or various students read the parts leading up to and after the acted scenes. Students participating in the acted scene should be set up prior to the time that the reading begins so they can just proceed with their acting and the flow of the story is not interrupted.

Activity #3

Tell students that prior to the class meeting after next they need to have read chapters 27-33 and to have completed the prereading work (previewing the study questions and doing the prereading vocabulary worksheet) for chapters 29-31 and 32-35. Give students any remaining class time to work on this assignment.

LESSON TEN

Objectives
1. To give students the opportunity to practice writing to persuade
2. To review events and character motivations from the novel
3. To give the teacher the opportunity to evaluate students' writing skills
4. To review the main ideas and events from chapters 23-28

Activity #1

Give students a few minutes to formulate answers for the study guide questions for chapters 23-28, and then discuss the answers to the questions in detail. Write the answers on the board or overhead transparency so students can have the correct answers for study purposes.

Activity #2

Distribute Writing Assignment #2. Discuss the directions in detail and give students ample time to complete the assignment.

WRITING ASSIGNMENT #2 - *The Adventures of Tom Sawyer*

PROMPT
For this assignment you may choose to be any character in the book except Huck Finn. You are to write a letter to Huck Finn in which you persuade him to stay with the Widow Douglas and become civilized. Use any arguments except the one Tom used (that he wouldn't let Huck in his gang if he didn't become civilized).

PREWRITING
First decide what character you would like to be -- Becky? Widow Douglas? Tom? Sid? Aunt Polly? Judge Thatcher? From whose point of view do you want to write your letter?

Think about the character you have chosen. Why would that person want Huck Finn to stay and become civilized? What possible advantages in becoming civilized would that person see for Huck? Make a list of all the reasons you can think of.

DRAFTING
Write an introductory paragraph in which you introduce the idea that you think Huck should stay and become civilized.

In the body of your letter, write one paragraph for each of the reasons you thought of as to why Huck should stay and become civilized. Fill out your paragraphs with examples and explanations of your reasons.

Write a concluding paragraph in which you give your final words to Huck and close your letter.

PROMPT
When you finish the rough draft of your paper, ask a student who sits near you to read it. After reading your rough draft, he/she should tell you what he/she liked best about your work, which parts were difficult to understand, and ways in which your work could be improved. Reread your paper considering your critic's comments, and make the corrections you think are necessary.

PROOFREADING
Do a final proofreading of your paper double-checking your grammar, spelling, organization, and the clarity of your ideas.

LESSON ELEVEN

Objectives
1. To review the main ideas and events from chapters 33-35
2. To review all of the vocabulary work done in this unit

Activity #1

Give students a few minutes to formulate answers for the study guide questions for chapters 33-35, and then discuss the answers to the questions in detail. Write the answers on the board or overhead transparency so students can have the correct answers for study purposes.

Activity #2

Choose one (or more) of the vocabulary review activities listed on the next page and spend your class period as directed in the activity. Some of the materials for these review activities are located in the Vocabulary Resources section in this unit.

LESSON TWELVE

Objectives
1. To review the main events and ideas from chapters 29-31
2. To read chapter 33 orally
5. To complete reading *Tom Sawyer*

Activity #1

Give students a few minutes to formulate answers for the study guide questions for chapters 29-31, and then discuss the answers to the questions in detail. Write the answers on the board or overhead transparency so students can have the correct answers for study purposes.

Activity #2

Have students read chapter 33 of *The Adventures of Tom Sawyer* out loud in class. Have a narrator or various students read the parts leading up to and after the acted scenes. Students participating in the acted scene should be set up prior to the time that the reading begins so they can just proceed with their acting and the flow of the story is not interrupted.

Activity #3

Tell students that prior to your next class meeting they should have read the remainder of the book *Tom Sawyer*. If time remains in this class period, students may begin this assignment.

VOCABULARY REVIEW ACTIVITIES

1. Divide your class into two teams and have an old-fashioned spelling or definition bee.

2. Give each of your students (or students in groups of two, three or four) a *Tom Sawyer* Vocabulary Word Search Puzzle. The person (group) to find all of the vocabulary words in the puzzle first wins.

3. Give students a *Tom Sawyer* Vocabulary Word Search Puzzle without the word list. The person or group to find the most vocabulary words in the puzzle wins.

4. Use a *Tom Sawyer* Vocabulary Crossword Puzzle. Put the puzzle onto a transparency on the overhead projector (so everyone can see it), and do the puzzle together as a class.

5. Give students a *Tom Sawyer* Vocabulary Matching Worksheet to do.

6. Divide your class into two teams. Use the *Tom Sawyer* vocabulary words with their letters jumbled as a word list. Student 1 from Team A faces off against Student 1 from Team B. You write the first jumbled word on the board. The first student (1A or 1B) to unscramble the word wins the chance for his/her team to score points. If 1A wins the jumble, go to student 2A and give him/her a definition. He/she must give you the correct spelling of the vocabulary word which fits that definition. If he/she does, Team A scores a point, and you give student 3A a definition for which you expect a correctly spelled matching vocabulary word. Continue giving Team A definitions until some team member makes an incorrect response. An incorrect response sends the game back to the jumbled-word face off, this time with students 2A and 2B. Instead of repeating giving definitions to the first few students of each team, continue with the student after the one who gave the last incorrect response on the team. For example, if Team B wins the jumbled-word face-off, and student 5B gave the last incorrect answer for Team B, you would start this round of definition questions with student 6B, and so on. The team with the most points wins!

7. Have students write a story in which they correctly use as many vocabulary words as possible. Have students read their compositions orally! Post the most original compositions on your bulletin board!

LESSONS THIRTEEN AND FOURTEEN

Objective

To discuss *Tom Sawyer* on interpretive and critical levels

Activity

Choose the questions from the Extra Discussion Questions/Writing Assignments which seem most appropriate for your students. A class discussion of these questions is most effective if students have been given the opportunity to formulate answers to the questions prior to the discussion. To this end, you may either have all the students formulate answers to all the questions, divide your class into groups and assign one or more questions to each group, or you could assign one question to each student in your class. The option you choose will make a difference in the amount of class time needed for this activity.

After students have had ample time to formulate answers to the questions, begin your class discussion of the questions and the ideas presented by the questions. Be sure students take notes during the discussion so they have information to study for the unit test.

EXTRA WRITING ASSIGNMENTS/DISCUSSION QUESTIONS - *Tom Sawyer*

<u>Interpretation</u>

1. From what point of view is *The Adventures of Tom Sawyer* written, and what effect does that have on the story?

2. Is the story of *The Adventures of Tom Sawyer* believable? Explain why or why not.

3. Where is the climax of the story? Explain your choice.

4. Are the characters in *The Adventures of Tom Sawyer* stereotypes? If so, explain the usefulness of employing stereotypes in the novel. If they are not, explain how they merit individuality.

5. What is the setting of the story? Could this story have been set in a different time and place and still have the same effect?

6. What are the main conflicts in the story and how are they resolved?

<u>Critical</u>

7. Compare and contrast Huck and Tom.

8. Are Tom's actions believably motivated? Explain why or why not.

9. Characterize Mark Twain's style of writing. How does it contribute to the value of the novel?

10. Does Tom change at all during the novel?

11. Find references to superstitions in the book. How do the superstitions affect our views of Tom and Huck?

12. Describe the relationship between Tom and Sid.

13. Describe the relationship between Becky and Tom.

14. What major coincidences occur in the book? Of what use are they?

15. What events occur at midnight?

16. What are the main stories in Tom's adventures?

17. What kind of a man is Mr. Dobbins? What does Twain gain by making him that way?

The Adventures of Tom Sawyer Extra Discussion Questions page 2

18. Give three examples of Twain's use of satire.

19. Give three examples of Twain's use of humor.

20. What messages are presented to the reader of this book?

21. Injun Joe is purely rotten through and through. What does this character add to the story?

22. Describe Muff Potter. what kind of a man is he?

23. What does Mr. Jones, the Welshman, add to the story?

24. What kinds of things does Tom do which are primarily associated with boyhood?

Personal Response

25. Did you enjoy reading *The Adventures of Tom Sawyer*? Why or why not?

26. Would you have liked to have been a part of The Adventures of Tom Sawyer's world? Explain why or why not.

27. Was Tom a "good boy"? Will he grow up to be a good man?

28. How would Tom define the word "hero"?

29. Was Aunt Polly a good parent? What makes a good parent?

30. What part of the book did you like the best? Why?

LESSON FIFTEEN

Objectives
    1. To prepare students for the oral reports about the nonfiction they have read
    2. To give students the opportunity to practice writing to inform
    3. To give the teacher the opportunity to evaluate students' writing skills

Activity
    Distribute Writing Assignment #3. Discuss the directions in detail and give students ample time to complete the assignment.

NOTE: While students are working on Writing Assignment #3, call individual students to your desk or some other private area for writing conferences based on the first two writing assignments. An evaluation form is included in this unit for your convenience. After discussing the students' writing and making suggestions to them, have them revise their first two writing assignments taking your suggestions into consideration. Be sure to tell students when their revisions will be due.

    When you grade the revisions, you might want to use an A-C-E scale (A=all corrections done well, C=some corrections done well, E=corrections done poorly or no corrections made). That speeds up grading time and still gives students credit for their efforts. A second writing conference would be ideal if you can make the time to do it.

LESSON SIXTEEN

Objectives
    1. To widen the breadth of students' knowledge about the topics discussed or
        touched upon in *The Adventures of Tom Sawyer*
    2. To check students' nonfiction reading assignments

Activity
    Ask each student to give a brief oral report about the nonfiction work he/she read for the nonfiction reading assignment. Your criteria for evaluating this report will vary depending on the level of your students. You may wish for students to give a complete report without using notes of any kind, or you may want students to read directly from a written report, or you may want to do something in between these two extremes. Just make students aware of your criteria in ample time for them to prepare their reports.

    Start with one student's report. After that, ask if anyone else in the class has read about a topic related to the first student's report. If no one has, choose another student at random. After each report, be sure to ask if anyone has a report related to the one just completed. That will help keep a continuity during the discussion of the reports.

WRITING ASSIGNMENT #3 - *The Adventures of Tom Sawyer*

PROMPT

You have read some nonfiction article(s) about topics related to *Tom Sawyer*. During our next class meeting you will have to give a little oral report sharing with the class the information you have read. This assignment is to help you prepare for that report.

Your assignment is to write a summary of the article(s) you read for the nonfiction reading assignment.

PREWRITING

Write down in a few words what the main topic of the article was. What main points did the article make about the topic? Jot those down. Make a few notes about what you thought of the article.

DRAFTING

Write one paragraph in which you introduce the main topic of the article and how it relates to *Tom Sawyer*.

In the body of your composition, tell the main points that the article made, and any supporting examples or explanations that were given.

Write one paragraph in which you tell what you thought about the article.

Bring your composition to a close with a concluding paragraph.

PROMPT

When you finish the rough draft of your paper, ask a student who sits near you to read it. After reading your rough draft, he/she should tell you what he/she liked best about your work, which parts were difficult to understand, and ways in which your work could be improved. Reread your paper considering your critic's comments, and make the corrections you think are necessary.

PROOFREADING

Do a final proofreading of your paper double-checking your grammar, spelling, organization, and the clarity of your ideas.

WRITING EVALUATION FORM - *The Adventures of Tom Sawyer*

Name _____ Date _____

      Grade _____

Circle One For Each Item:

Grammar:		excellent	good	fair	poor

Spelling:		excellent	good	fair	poor

Punctuation:		excellent	good	fair	poor

Legibility:		excellent	good	fair	poor

Strengths:

Weaknesses:

Comments/Suggestions:

LESSONS SEVENTEEN AND EIGHTEEN

Objectives
1. To tie together the "fact" and "fiction" elements of the story
2. To give students some practical application related to *The Adventures of Tom Sawyer*
3. To show students how to make a fun day without the "bad" things that are so often associated with teen parties

Activity #1

Explain to your class that they are going to recreate a modern-day, old-fashioned picnic. That sounds contradictory, but it actually is possible to do. Students should plan carnival-type activities (three-legged races, knock over the bottles, get the ball into the basket, pie eating contest, a cake walk, a dance contest, etc.) that are traditionally associated with old-fashioned picnics, but they may add a modern-day twist to the activities. Use modern music and modern dances for the dance contest. Ask your local retailers for donations for prizes--things that kids would want today.

Have the entire class (with your help) decide when and where to have the **Tom Sawyer Day Picnic.**

Divide your class into three groups: one for activities, one for prizes, and one for food.

Activities Group: Plan activities, make the rules for the games, and make sure the necessary equipment is ready and available on the Tom Sawyer Day.

Prize Group: Find out from the Activities Group how many prizes you will need to acquire. Brainstorm a list of things that would make good prizes, contact your local retailers to see if anyone would give donations to your project, and make sure the prizes are available on the Tom Sawyer Day.

Food Group: Decide what kinds of foods and drinks to have on Tom Sawyer Day and make sure they are prepared and available. Don't forget paper products and trash cans.

Use Lessons Seventeen and Eighteen for students to plan their event.

LESSON NINETEEN

Objective
To review the main ideas and events from the novel *The Adventures of Tom Sawyer*

Activity
Choose one or more of the review activities on the following page and spend your class time as directed there.

REVIEW GAMES/ACTIVITIES - *The Adventures of Tom Sawyer*

1. Ask the class to make up a unit test for *The Adventures of Tom Sawyer*. The test should have 4 sections: matching, true/false, short answer, and essay. Students may use 1/2 period to make the test and then swap papers and use the other 1/2 class period to take a test a classmate has devised. (open book) You may want to use the unit test included in this unit or take questions from the students' unit tests to formulate your own test.

2. Take 1/2 period for students to make up true and false questions (including the answers). Collect the papers and divide the class into two teams. Draw a big tic-tac-toe board on the chalk board. Make one team X and one team O. Ask questions to each side, giving each student one turn. If the question is answered correctly, that students' team's letter (X or O) is placed in the box. If the answer is incorrect, no mark is placed in the box. The object is to get three marks in a row like tic-tac-toe. You may want to keep track of the number of games won for each team.

3. Take 1/2 period for students to make up questions (true/false and short answer). Collect the questions. Divide the class into two teams. You'll alternate asking questions to individual members of teams A & B (like in a spelling bee). The question keeps going from A to B until it is correctly answered, then a new question is asked. A correct answer does not allow the team to get another question. Correct answers are +2 points; incorrect answers are -1 point.

4. Have students pair up and quiz each other from their study guides and class notes.

5. Give students a *Tom Sawyer* crossword puzzle to complete.

6. Divide your class into two teams. Use the *Tom Sawyer* crossword words with their letters jumbled as a word list. Student 1 from Team A faces off against Student 1 from Team B. You write the first jumbled word on the board. The first student (1A or 1B) to unscramble the word wins the chance for his/her team to score points. If 1A wins the jumble, go to student 2A and give him/her a clue. He/she must give you the correct word which matches that clue. If he/she does, Team A scores a point, and you give student 3A a clue for which you expect another correct response. Continue giving Team A clues until some team member makes an incorrect response. An incorrect response sends the game back to the jumbled-word face off, this time with students 2A and 2B. Instead of repeating giving clues to the first few students of each team, continue with the student after the one who gave the last incorrect response on the team. For example, if Team B wins the jumbled-word face-off, and student 5B gave the last incorrect answer for Team B, you would start this round of clue questions with student 6B, and so on. The team with the most points wins!

LESSON TWENTY

Objective
To test the students understanding of the main ideas and themes in *The Adventures of Tom Sawyer*

Activity #1
Distribute the unit tests. Go over the instructions in detail and allow the students the entire class period to complete the exam.

NOTES ABOUT THE UNIT TESTS IN THIS UNIT:

There are 5 different unit tests which follow.

There are two short answer tests which are based primarily on facts from the novel. The answer key short answer unit test 1 follows the student test. The answer key for short answer test 2 follows the student short answer unit test 2.

There is one advanced short answer unit test. It is based on the extra discussion questions and quotations. Use the matching key for short answer unit test 2 to check the matching section of the advanced short answer unit test. There is no key for the short answer questions and quotations. The answers will be based on the discussions you have had during class.

There are two multiple choice unit tests. Following the two unit tests, you will find an answer sheet on which students should mark their answers. The same answer sheet should be used for both tests; however, students' answers will be different for each test. Following the students' answer sheet for the multiple choice tests you will find your answer keys.

The short answer tests have a vocabulary section. You should choose 10 of the vocabulary words from this unit, read them orally and have the students write them down. Then, either have students write a definition or use the words in sentences.

Use these words for the vocabulary section of the advanced short answer unit test:

abstain	caricature	condescend	derision
ingenious	magnanimous	pallid	precarious
prodigious	tedious	unpalatable	wary

Activity #2
Collect all test papers and assigned books prior to the end of the class period.

UNIT TESTS

SHORT ANSWER UNIT TEST 1 - *The Adventures of Tom Sawyer*

I. Matching/Identify

____ 1. Aunt Polly   A. Went to island with Huck and Tom

____ 2. Alfred   B. Tom's half-brother

____ 3. Sid   C. Teacher

____ 4. Huck   D. _____'s Island

____ 5. Joe   E. Tom's guardian

____ 6. Becky   F. Murderer

____ 7. Mary   G. Tom's girl cousin

____ 8. Dobbins   H. Son of the town drunk

____ 9. Muff Potter   I. Cat

____ 10. Jackson   J. Drunk accused of murder

____ 11. Peter   K. New Boy

____ 12. Injun Joe   L. Engaged to Tom

II. Short Answer

1. Why does Tom live with his Aunt Polly?

2. What was Tom's Saturday job for punishment? How did he escape doing it? What did he do instead?

3. How did Tom get his ten yellow tickets?

The Adventures of Tom Sawyer Short Answer Unit Test 1 Page 2

4. What did Tom and Becky do at school during recess?

5. Where did Tom go that night he left Huck and Joe on the island?

6. What was Tom's "dream"?

7. What noble thing did Tom do?

8 Give three examples of superstition from *The Adventures of Tom Sawyer*.

9. Against whom was the revenge job about which Injun Joe spoke?

10. How were Becky and Tom saved?

11. What happened to Injun Joe?

12. How did Tom convince Huck to stay with the Widow Douglas?

The Adventures of Tom Sawyer Short Answer Unit Test 1 Page 3

III. Composition
    Keith Neilson wrote, "*Tom Sawyer*" is a fun book, a vital, nostalgic evocation of a time of life, boyhood, and a place and period, nineteenth-century small-town America. Defend his statement using examples from the novel.

The Adventures of Tom Sawyer Short Answer Unit Test 1 Page 4

IV. Vocabulary

Listen to the vocabulary words and write them down. Go back later and fill in the correct definition for each word.

1.

2.

3.

4.

5.

6.

7.

8.

9.

10.

KEY: SHORT ANSWER UNIT TEST #1 - *The Adventures of Tom Sawyer*

I. Matching/Identify

_E_	1. Aunt Polly	A.	Went to island with Huck and Tom
_K_	2. Alfred	B.	Tom's half-brother
_B_	3. Sid	C.	Teacher
_H_	4. Huck	D.	_____'s Island
_A_	5. Joe	E.	Tom's guardian
_L_	6. Becky	F.	Murderer
_G_	7. Mary	G.	Tom's girl cousin
_C_	8. Dobbins	H.	Son of the town drunk
_J_	9. Muff Potter	I.	Cat
_D_	10. Jackson	J.	Drunk accused of murder
_I_	11. Peter	K.	New Boy
_F_	12. Injun Joe	L.	Engaged to Tom

II. Short Answer

1. Why does Tom live with his Aunt Polly?
    He lives with her because his parents are dead.

2. What was Tom's Saturday job for punishment? How did he escape doing it? What did he do instead?
    He was supposed to whitewash the fence, but he got the boys in the neighborhood to do it for him by telling them what fun whitewashing is and how not just everyone can do it. Tom just sat back and watched and collected "trading stuff" the boys gave him to let them whitewash the fence.

3. How did Tom get his ten yellow tickets?
   He didn't earn them by memorizing bible verses, he traded stuff with other kids to get his tickets.

4. What did Tom and Becky do at school during recess?
   They became engaged.

5. Where did Tom go that night he left Huck and Joe on the island?
   He sneaked away from the island and went to Aunt Polly's house to see what was going on there.

6. What was Tom's "dream"?
   His dream was what he really saw the night he came back to Aunt Polly's house.

7. What noble thing did Tom do?
   He took the blame for tearing the teacher's book in order to spare Becky.

8. Give three examples of superstition from *The Adventures of Tom Sawyer*.
   There were many examples. Some are:
   - Bad things happen in haunted houses on Fridays
   - Rats are a sure sign of trouble
   - Witches interfered with the marble spell
   - Dead cats cure warts
   - You find treasure where the dead limb's shadow points at midnight

9. Against whom was the revenge job about which Injun Joe spoke?
   It was supposed to be against the Widow Douglas.

10. How were Becky and Tom saved?
    Tom went exploring and saw a patch of daylight. He followed the daylight and found a small exit near the Mississippi River. Tom hailed the people on a skiff and they took Becky and Tom towards home.

11. What happened to Injun Joe?
    He got trapped in the cave and died.

12. How did Tom convince Huck to stay with the Widow Douglas?
    He told Huck he couldn't be in the gang unless he stayed with the widow and became respectable.

IV. Vocabulary: Choose ten of the vocabulary words to dictate to your class.

SHORT ANSWER UNIT TEST 2 - *The Adventures of Tom Sawyer*

I. Matching/Identify

____ 1. Aunt Polly   A. Tom's girl cousin

____ 2. Alfred   B. Engaged to Tom

____ 3. Sid   C. _____'s Island

____ 4. Huck   D. Teacher

____ 5. Joe   E. Tom's guardian

____ 6. Becky   F. Murderer

____ 7. Mary   G. Cat

____ 8. Dobbins   H. Son of the town drunk

____ 9. Muff Potter   I. Went to island with Huck and Tom

____ 10. Jackson   J. Drunk accused of murder

____ 11. Peter   K. New Boy

____ 12. Injun Joe   L. Tom's half-brother

Tom Sawyer Short Answer Unit Test 2 Page 2

II. Short Answer

1. List at least three of the tricks Tom played on people in the early part of the book.

2. Give at least two examples of things Tom did that were typical, "little boy" kinds of things to do.

3. What did Huck and Tom see in the graveyard?

4. Why did Tom bring things to Muff Potter in jail?

5. Why did the villagers not tar and feather Injun Joe?

6. What do we learn about Tom from his sneaky visit back to Aunt Polly's house?

Tom Sawyer Short Answer Unit Test 2 Page 3

7. Describe Tom's relationship with Becky.

8. Why did Tom tell the truth about Injun Joe?

9. Give at least two examples of superstition from the book.

10. How did Tom and Becky get lost in the cave?

11. How were Becky and Tom saved?

Tom Sawyer Short Answer Unit Test 2 Page 4

III. Composition

    Pick five scenes from the book. Describe each briefly, and tell what we learn about Tom's character from each scene.

The Adventures of Tom Sawyer Short Answer Unit Test 2 Page 5

IV. Vocabulary

Listen to the vocabulary words and write them down. Go back later and fill in the correct definition for each word.

1.

2.

3.

4.

5.

6.

7.

8.

9.

10.

KEY: SHORT ANSWER UNIT TEST 2 *The Adventures of Tom Sawyer*

I. Matching (Use this matching key also for the Advanced Short Answer Unit Test)

_E_	1. Aunt Polly	A.	Tom's girl cousin
_K_	2. Alfred	B.	Engaged to Tom
_L_	3. Sid	C.	_____'s Island
_H_	4. Huck	D.	Teacher
_I_	5. Joe	E.	Tom's guardian
_B_	6. Becky	F.	Murderer
_A_	7. Mary	G.	Cat
_D_	8. Dobbins	H.	Son of the town drunk
_J_	9. Muff Potter	I.	Went to island with Huck and Tom
_C_	10. Jackson	J.	Drunk accused of murder
_G_	11. Peter	K.	New Boy
_F_	12. Injun Joe	L.	Tom's half-brother

II. Short Answer

1. List at least three of the tricks Tom played on people in the early part of the book.

    When Aunt Polly was about to spank him, he told her to look behind her, and when she did, he ran away. Tom wasn't supposed to go swimming, so to fool Aunt Polly, he had taken his shirt off, gone swimming and then resown it. Tom was supposed to whitewash the fence, but he got the boys in the neighborhood to do it for him by telling them what fun whitewashing is and how not just everyone can do it. Tom just sat back and watched and collected "trading stuff" the boys gave him to let them whitewash the fence. Tom traded stuff for yellow tickets instead of learning the Bible verses. There are many other correct answers; these are just a few examples.)

2. Give at least two examples of things Tom did that were typical, "little boy" kinds of things to do.
   He had passed the time in church watching a pinch-bug in the aisle, and its conflict with a loose poodle. He was proud of the fact that he had lost a tooth and could spit through the gap in his remaining teeth. Tom and Joe played with a tick on a slate during school. Tom decided to become a pirate. (There are other correct answers; these are just some examples.)

3. What did Huck and Tom see in the graveyard?
   Tom and Huck saw these three men robbing a grave. Injun Joe saw the opportunity to kill Dr. Robinson and did so, blaming the drunken Muff Potter, who couldn't remember enough to say otherwise. Tom and Huck witnessed the whole incident.

4. Why did Tom bring things to Muff Potter in jail?
   It helped to ease his conscience; he felt guilty for not speaking out to proclaim Muff's innocence.

5. Why did the villagers not tar and feather Injun Joe?
   They were all afraid of him; no one would lead the mob.

6. What do we learn about Tom from his sneaky visit back to Aunt Polly's house?
   As a kid, he is enjoying his notoriety. He doesn't have the maturity to recognize the fact that he is making Aunt Polly suffer needlessly.

7. Describe Tom's relationship with Becky.
   They're good friends and even become "engaged" at one point in the story. They bring out the best and worst in each other. Tom is willing to take Becky's punishment, and he acts in a more mature fashion in the cave when he and Becky are lost than at any other point in the book. However, his feelings for her also cause him to do several childish acts as well.

8. Why did Tom tell the truth about Injun Joe?
   His conscience was killing him; he couldn't stand to see an innocent person (Muff) punished for someone else's crime.

9. Give at least two examples of superstition from the book.
   The boys stopped treasure hunting because it was Friday, and bad things happen in haunted houses on Fridays. Also, Huck had a dream about rats, and rats are a sure sign of trouble. (There are many other acceptable answers.)

10. How did Tom and Becky get lost in the cave?
    They went "discovering" and lost their way.

11. How were Becky and Tom saved?
    Tom went exploring and saw a patch of daylight. He followed the daylight and found a small exit near the Mississippi River. Tom hailed the people on a skiff and they took Becky and Tom towards home.

III. Composition: Answers will vary.

IV. Vocabulary: Choose ten vocabulary words to dictate to your students for this part of the test.

ADVANCED SHORT ANSWER UNIT TEST - *The Adventures of Tom Sawyer*

I. Matching

___ 1. Aunt Polly   A. Tom's girl cousin

___ 2. Alfred   B. Engaged to Tom

___ 3. Sid   C. _____'s Island

___ 4. Huck   D. Teacher

___ 5. Joe   E. Tom's guardian

___ 6. Becky   F. Murderer

___ 7. Mary   G. Cat

___ 8. Dobbins   H. Son of the town drunk

___ 9. Muff Potter   I. Went to island with Huck and Tom

___ 10. Jackson   J. Drunk accused of murder

___ 11. Peter   K. New Boy

___ 12. Injun Joe   L. Tom's half-brother

II. Short Answer
1. Compare and contrast Tom and Huck.

2. Describe the relationship between Becky and Tom.

The Adventures of Tom Sawyer Advanced Short Answer Unit Test Page 2

3. Give three examples of Twain's use of humor.

4. Where is the climax of the story? Defend your choice using examples from the text.

5. Why is the character of Injun Joe important in the book?

6. List five different scenes from Tom's adventures. Describe each briefly and tell what we learn about Tom's character from each scene.
   a.

   b.

   c.

   d.

   e.

The Adventures of Tom Sawyer Advanced Short Answer Unit Test Page 3

III. Composition

Marion P. Thayer said, "It [*The Adventures of Tom Sawyer*] transcends time and place and becomes universal in its revelation of human nature and its creation of a boy world, with fears, fantasies, and limited viewpoint." Defend this statement using specific examples from the text.

The Adventures of Tom Sawyer Advanced Short Answer Unit Test Page 4

IV. Vocabulary

    Write down the vocabulary words you are given. Go back later and use all of those vocabulary words in a composition relating to *The Adventures of Tom Sawyer*.

MULTIPLE CHOICE UNIT TEST 1 - *The Adventures of Tom Sawyer*

I. Matching/Identify

____ 1. Aunt Polly   A. Went to island with Huck and Tom

____ 2. Alfred   B. Tom's half-brother

____ 3. Sid   C. Teacher

____ 4. Huck   D. _____'s Island

____ 5. Joe   E. Tom's guardian

____ 6. Becky   F. Murderer

____ 7. Mary   G. Tom's girl cousin

____ 8. Dobbins   H. Son of the town drunk

____ 9. Muff Potter   I. Cat

____ 10. Jackson   J. Drunk accused of murder

____ 11. Peter   K. New Boy

____ 12. Injun Joe   L. Engaged to Tom

The Adventures of Tom Sawyer Multiple Choice Unit Test 1 Page 2

II. Multiple Choice
1. Which of these was not a trick Tom played on people in the early part of the book.
    a. When Aunt Polly was about to spank him, he told her to look behind her, and when she did, he ran away.
    b. Tom wasn't supposed to go swimming, so to fool Aunt Polly, he had taken his shirt off, gone swimming and then resown it.
    c. Tom was supposed to whitewash the fence, but he got the boys in the neighborhood to do it for him by telling them what fun whitewashing is and how not just everyone can do it. Tom just sat back and watched and collected "trading stuff" the boys gave him to let them whitewash the fence.
    d. Tom put a spider in the sugar bowl.

2. What is not one of the things Tom did that was a typical, "little boy" kind of thing to do.
    a. He waved a spider at Becky and then pulled all its legs off and squashed the body.
    b. He had passed the time in church watching a pinch-bug in the aisle, and its conflict with a loose poodle.
    c. He was proud of the fact that he had lost a tooth and could spit through the gap in his remaining teeth.
    d. Tom and Joe played with a tick on a slate during school.

3. What did Huck and Tom see in the graveyard?
    a. Tom and Huck saw these three men robbing a grave.
    b. Tom and Huck witnessed a murder.
    c. Tom and Huck saw a Spaniard chasing a drunk man.
    d. a & b

4. Why did Tom bring things to Muff Potter in jail?
    a. He was just playing a game, bringing Muff useless stuff like string, a spoon, and a pointless pencil with some tree bark on which to write a farewell note--much the same as we later see him do again to Jim in *The Adventures of Huckleberry Finn*.
    b. It helped to ease his conscience; he felt guilty for not speaking out to proclaim Muff's innocence.
    c. Aunt Polly made him do it because she felt sorry for Muff Potter.
    d. He had been in so much trouble lately, he thought he'd better do something to show everyone he was really a "good boy."

The Adventures of Tom Sawyer Multiple Choice Unit Test 1 Page 3

5. Why did the villagers not tar and feather Injun Joe?
    a. They couldn't catch him.
    b. He was such a big man it would have been physically impossible.
    c. They were all afraid of him; no one would lead the mob.
    d. All of the above

6. What do we learn about Tom from his sneaky visit back to Aunt Polly's house?
    a. He has no loyalties whatsoever; none to the boys and none to Aunt Polly.
    b. As a kid, he is enjoying his notoriety. He doesn't have the maturity to recognize the fact that he is making Aunt Polly suffer needlessly.
    c. Tom is vengeful. He could tell Aunt Polly he is alive, but he decides not to because he wants her to feel miserable for a while, like she has made him miserable with his punishments.
    d. All of the above

7. Describe Tom's relationship with Becky.
    a. They have a typical sibling relationship.
    b. Becky chases Tom and tries her darndest to get him interested in her, but he is more interested in bugs, spiders, and buried treasure than girls.
    c. Tom is jealous of her close family relationships and that she has a "real" family. He does everything he can to annoy her.
    d. They're good friends and even become "engaged" at one point in the story. They bring out the best and worst in each other.

8. Why did Tom tell the truth about Injun Joe?
    a. He didn't mean to, it just slipped out.
    b. He didn't have any choice
    c. His conscience was killing him; he couldn't stand to see an innocent person punished for someone else's crime.
    d. Huck let it slip out first, so Tom had to "fess up," too.

9. Which of these is an example of superstition from the book?
    a. The boys stopped treasure hunting because it was Friday, and bad things happen in haunted houses on Fridays.
    b. Tom finds a snakeskin in the cave and knows then that he and Becky are doomed because snakeskins are a sign of bad luck, but then he finds a dead bat and knows that everything will be okay since dead bats are a sign of good luck and are far more powerful than snakeskins.
    c. Tom and Huck find a bone above the ground in the graveyard. Tom tells Huck that's a sure sign that there's going to be a murder.
    d. Becky's candle flickers and goes out in the cave, a sign that the cave is haunted.

The Adventures of Tom Sawyer Multiple Choice Unit Test 1 Page 4

10. Why did Injun Joe kill the doctor?
    - A. It was to settle an old score. Five years earlier, the doctor had insulted Injun Joe and refused to give him food. Injun Joe was still angry.
    - B. The doctor was refusing to pay them for their work.
    - C. Someone else in town who didn't like the doctor had paid Injun Joe to do it.
    - D. Injun Joe got superstitious at the last minute. He didn't want anyone to find out he was involved with digging up the grave, so he decided to kill the witnesses. Unfortunately, he only managed to kill one of them.

11. What plan did Tom and Huck make for finding the real treasure?
    - A. They would sneak into the alley at night. While Huck would break in to Number Two, Tom would keep watch.
    - B. They would sneak into the alley at night. While Tom would break in to Number Two, Huck would keep watch.
    - C. They would let Joe in on their plans. Joe and Huck would keep watch while Tom broke in and took the money.
    - D. They would masquerade as cleaning boys. They would go into the room in broad daylight, while the occupants were out, and take the treasure.

12. What happened to Injun Joe?
    - A. He escaped and was never seen again.
    - B. He was arrested and sent to jail.
    - C. He got trapped in the cave and died.
    - D. No one was ever sure. He just disappeared.

The Adventures of Tom Sawyer Multiple Choice Unit Test 1 Page 5

III. Composition

    Marion P. Thayer said, "Twain tells excellent stories, accurately describes nature, and warmly satirizes accepted institutions in a style that is noteworthy for its clearness and readability." Defend this statement using examples from the story *The Adventures of Tom Sawyer*.

The Adventures of Tom Sawyer Multiple Choice Unit Test 1 Page 6

IV. Vocabulary

___ 1. Covet   a. face

___ 2. Prodigious   b. ridicule

___ 3. Resolution   c. calmed; satisfied; pacified

___ 4. Countenance   d. anxiously

___ 5. Magnanimous   e. burn; scorch

___ 6. Assent   f. agreement

___ 7. Tyranny   g. impressively great

___ 8. Sear   h. dangerously lacking in security or stability

___ 9. Apprehensively i. a ruler's unjust use of power

___ 10. Wary   j. courageously noble

___ 11. Unpalatable   k. inflicted a heavy blow upon

___ 12. Smote   l. thinking

___ 13. Appeased   m. reprimand

___ 14. Derision   n. want

___ 15. Mutual   o. determination

___ 16. Dauntless   p. possessed in common

___ 17. Pervading   q. cautious

___ 18. Upbraid   r. present throughout

___ 19. Precarious   s. unacceptable to the mind or senses

___ 20. Cogitating   t. fearless

MULTIPLE CHOICE UNIT TEST 2 - *The Adventures of Tom Sawyer*

I. Matching

____ 1. Aunt Polly   A. Tom's girl cousin

____ 2. Alfred   B. Engaged to Tom

____ 3. Sid   C. _____'s Island

____ 4. Huck   D. Teacher

____ 5. Joe   E. Tom's guardian

____ 6. Becky   F. Murderer

____ 7. Mary   G. Cat

____ 8. Dobbins   H. Son of the town drunk

____ 9. Muff Potter   I. Went to island with Huck and Tom

____ 10. Jackson   J. Drunk accused of murder

____ 11. Peter   K. New Boy

____ 12. Injun Joe   L. Tom's half-brother

The Adventures of Tom Sawyer Multiple Choice Unit Test 2 Page 2

II. Multiple Choice

1. Which of these was not a trick Tom played on people in the early part of the book.
    a. Tom was supposed to whitewash the fence, but he got the boys in the neighborhood to do it for him by telling them what fun whitewashing is and how not just everyone can do it. Tom just sat back and watched and collected "trading stuff" the boys gave him to let them whitewash the fence.
    b. Tom wasn't supposed to go swimming, so to fool Aunt Polly, he had taken his shirt off, gone swimming and then resown it.
    c. Tom put a spider in the sugar bowl.
    d. When Aunt Polly was about to spank him, he told her to look behind her, and when she did, he ran away.

2. Which isn't an example of something Tom did that was a typical "little boy" kind of thing.
    a. He was proud of the fact that he had lost a tooth and could spit through the gap in his remaining teeth.
    b. He had passed the time in church watching a pinch-bug in the aisle, and its conflict with a loose poodle.
    c. Tom and Joe played with a tick on a slate during school.
    d. He waved a spider at Becky and then pulled all its legs off and squished the body.

3. What did Huck and Tom see in the graveyard?
    a. Tom and Huck saw these three men robbing a grave.
    b. Tom and Huck saw a Spaniard chasing a drunk man.
    c. Tom and Huck witnessed a murder.
    d. a & c

4. Why did Tom bring things to Muff Potter in jail?
    a. He was just playing a game, bringing Muff useless stuff like string, a spoon, and a pointless pencil with some tree bark on which to write a farewell note--much the same as we later see him do again to Jim in *The Adventures of Huckleberry Finn*.
    b. Aunt Polly made him do it because she felt sorry for Muff Potter.
    c. It helped to ease his conscience; he felt guilty for not speaking out to proclaim Muff's innocence.
    d. He had been in so much trouble lately, he thought he'd better do something to show everyone he was really a "good boy."

The Adventures of Tom Sawyer Multiple Choice Unit Test 2 Page 3

5. Why did the villagers not tar and feather Injun Joe?
    a. They couldn't catch him.
    b. They were all afraid of him; no one would lead the mob.
    c. He was such a big man it would have been physically impossible.
    d. All of the above

6. What do we learn about Tom from his sneaky visit back to Aunt Polly's house?
    a. He has no loyalties whatsoever; none to the boys and none to Aunt Polly.
    b. Tom is vengeful. He could tell Aunt Polly he is alive, but he decides not to because he wants her to feel miserable for a while, like she has made him miserable with his punishments.
    c. As a kid, he is enjoying his notoriety. He doesn't have the maturity to recognize the fact that he is making Aunt Polly suffer needlessly.
    d. All of the above

7. Describe Tom's relationship with Becky.
    a. They're good friends and even become "engaged" at one point in the story. They bring out the best and worst in each other.
    b. Becky chases Tom and tries her darndest to get him interested in her, but he is more interested in bugs, spiders, and buried treasure than girls.
    c. Tom is jealous of her close family relationships and that she has a "real" family. He does everything he can to annoy her.
    d. They have a typical sibling relationship.

8. Why did Tom tell the truth about Injun Joe?
    a. He didn't mean to, it just slipped out.
    b. He didn't have any choice
    c. Huck let it slip out first, so Tom had to "fess up," too.
    d. His conscience was killing him; he couldn't stand to see an innocent person punished for someone else's crime.

9. Which of these is an example of superstition from the book?
    a. Tom and Huck find a bone above the ground in the graveyard. Tom tells Huck that's a sure sign that there's going to be a murder.
    b. Tom finds a snakeskin in the cave and knows then that he and Becky are doomed because snakeskins are a sign of bad luck, but then he finds a dead bat and knows that everything will be okay since dead bats are a sign of good luck and are far more powerful than snakeskins.
    c. The boys stopped treasure hunting because it was Friday, and bad things happen in haunted houses on Fridays.
    d. Becky's candle flickers and goes out in the cave, a sign that the cave is haunted.

The Adventures of Tom Sawyer Multiple Choice Unit Test 2 Page 2

II. Multiple Choice
1. Which of these was not a trick Tom played on people in the early part of the book.
    a. Tom was supposed to whitewash the fence, but he got the boys in the neighborhood to do it for him by telling them what fun whitewashing is and how not just everyone can do it. Tom just sat back and watched and collected "trading stuff" the boys gave him to let them whitewash the fence.
    b. Tom wasn't supposed to go swimming, so to fool Aunt Polly, he had taken his shirt off, gone swimming and then resown it.
    c. Tom put a spider in the sugar bowl.
    d. When Aunt Polly was about to spank him, he told her to look behind her, and when she did, he ran away.

2. Which isn't an example of something Tom did that was a typical "little boy" kind of thing.
    a. He was proud of the fact that he had lost a tooth and could spit through the gap in his remaining teeth.
    b. He had passed the time in church watching a pinch-bug in the aisle, and its conflict with a loose poodle.
    c. Tom and Joe played with a tick on a slate during school.
    d. He waved a spider at Becky and then pulled all its legs off and squished the body.

3. What did Huck and Tom see in the graveyard?
    a. Tom and Huck saw these three men robbing a grave.
    b. Tom and Huck saw a Spaniard chasing a drunk man.
    c. Tom and Huck witnessed a murder.
    d. a & c

4. Why did Tom bring things to Muff Potter in jail?
    a. He was just playing a game, bringing Muff useless stuff like string, a spoon, and a pointless pencil with some tree bark on which to write a farewell note--much the same as we later see him do again to Jim in *The Adventures of Huckleberry Finn*.
    b. Aunt Polly made him do it because she felt sorry for Muff Potter.
    c. It helped to ease his conscience; he felt guilty for not speaking out to proclaim Muff's innocence.
    d. He had been in so much trouble lately, he thought he'd better do something to show everyone he was really a "good boy."

The Adventures of Tom Sawyer Multiple Choice Unit Test 2 Page 5

III. Composition

    The Adventures of Tom Sawyer was written well over a hundred years ago. Why do people still read it? What makes this book a "classic" that is still read while thousands of other books have long been out of print?

The Adventures of Tom Sawyer Multiple Choice Unit Test 2 Page 6

IV. Vocabulary

___ 1. Averted   a. stop doing something by one's own choice

___ 2. Tyranny   b. dangerously lacking in security or stability

___ 3. Precarious   c. courageously noble

___ 4. Magnanimous   d. face

___ 5. Perplexed   e. anxiously

___ 6. Covet   f. stimulated; sharpened

___ 7. Imperishable   g. lower oneself to the position of inferiors

___ 8. Apprehensively   h. amazed with mixed emotions of reverence, respect and dread

___ 9. Whetted   i. puzzled; uncertain

___ 10. Sear   j. pale; dull; lifeless

___ 11. Warily   k. turned away

___ 12. Countenance   l. agree to something

___ 13. Consent   m. indestrictable

___ 14. Awed   n. burn; scorch

___ 15. Eloquent   o. clever, inventive

___ 16. Ingenious   p. cautiously

___ 17. Impaired   q. characterized by persuasive, powerful or moving discourse

___ 18. Condescend   r. damaged, diminished in strength

___ 19. Abstain   s. want

___ 20. Pallid   t. a ruler's unjust use of power

ANSWER SHEET - *The Adventures of Tom Sawyer*
Multiple Choice Unit Tests

I. Matching	II. Multiple Choice	IV. Vocabulary
1. ___	1. ___	1. ___
2. ___	2. ___	2. ___
3. ___	3. ___	3. ___
4. ___	4. ___	4. ___
5. ___	5. ___	5. ___
6. ___	6. ___	6. ___
7. ___	7. ___	7. ___
8. ___	8. ___	8. ___
9. ___	9. ___	9. ___
10. ___	10. ___	10. ___
11. ___	11. ___	11. ___
12. ___	12. ___	12. ___
		13. ___
		14. ___
		15. ___
		16. ___
		17. ___
		18. ___
		19. ___
		20. ___

ANSWER KEY - *Tom Sawyer*
Multiple Choice Unit Tests

Answers to Unit Test 1 are in the left column. Answers to Unit Test 2 are in the right column.

I. Matching	II. Multiple Choice	IV. Vocabulary
1. E E	1. D C	1. N K
2. K K	2. A D	2. G T
3. B L	3. D D	3. O B
4. H H	4. B C	4. A C
5. A I	5. C B	5. J I
6. L B	6. B C	6. F S
7. G A	7. D A	7. I M
8. C D	8. C D	8. E E
9. J J	9. A C	9. D F
10. D C	10. A B	10. Q N
11. I G	11. B C	11. S P
12. F F	12. C D	12. K D
		13. C L
		14. B H
		15. P Q
		16. T O
		17. R R
		18. M G
		19. H A
		20. L J

UNIT RESOURCE MATERIALS

BULLETIN BOARD IDEAS - *The Adventures of Tom Sawyer*

1. Save one corner of the board for the best of students' *The Adventures of Tom Sawyer* writing assignments.

2. Take one of the word search puzzles from the extra activities section and with a marker copy it over in a large size on the bulletin board. Write the clue words to find to one side. Invite students prior to and after class to find the words and circle them on the bulletin board.

3. Write several of the most significant quotations from the book onto the board on brightly colored paper.

4. Make a bulletin board listing the vocabulary words for this unit. As you complete sections of the novel and discuss the vocabulary for each section, write the definitions on the bulletin board. (If your board is one students face frequently, it will help them learn the words.)

5. Do a bulletin board about alcohol abuse. Be sure to include hotline numbers. Your guidance office may have materials you can use for this board.)

6. Do a bulletin board about superstitions. Title the board SUPERSTITIONS and invite students to write up all the superstitions they can think of on the board. Post pictures of things that represent superstitions -- like black cats, ladders, etc.

7. Title the board TOM SAWYER: A BOYHOOD WORLD OF TREASURES. Put up pictures of a cave, treasure, a white fence, an island, the Mississippi River, a boy and a girl holding hands, pirates, a tick, a little boat, a tooth, a poodle, a cat, a graveyard, etc.

8. Make a huge "book" and title it "*The Adventures of Tom Sawyer* by Mark Twain." All around it put words and pictures relating to what is in the story. For example you could use pirates, cave, murder, treasure, love, humor, satire, adventure, pranks, island, friendship, suspense, etc.

EXTRA ACTIVITIES

One of the difficulties in teaching a novel is that all students don't read at the same speed. One student who likes to read may take the book home and finish it in a day or two. Sometimes a few students finish the in-class assignments early. The problem, then, is finding suitable extra activities for students.

The best thing I've found is to keep a little library in the classroom. For this unit on *The Adventures of Tom Sawyer,* you might check out from the school library other related books and articles about superstitions, treasure hunting, caves and caverns, pirates, alcohol abuse, nature, adventure, etc. Other books, short stories or humorous sketches by Mark Twain would also be appropriate.

Other things you may keep on hand are puzzles. We have made some relating directly to *The Adventures of Tom Sawyer* for you. Feel free to duplicate them.

Some students may like to draw. You might devise a contest or allow some extra-credit grade for students who draw characters or scenes from *The Adventures of Tom Sawyer*. Note, too, that if the students do not want to keep their drawings you may pick up some extra bulletin board materials this way. If you have a contest and you supply the prize (a CD or something like that perhaps), you could, possibly, make the drawing itself a non-refundable entry fee.

The pages which follow contain games, puzzles and worksheets. The keys, when appropriate, immediately follow the puzzle or worksheet. There are two main groups of activities: one group for the unit; that is, generally relating to *The Adventures of Tom Sawyer* text, and another group of activities related strictly to *The Adventures of Tom Sawyer* vocabulary.

Directions for these games, puzzles and worksheets are self-explanatory. The object here is to provide you with extra materials you may use in any way you choose.

MORE ACTIVITIES - *The Adventures of Tom Sawyer*

1. Use some of the related topics (noted earlier for an in-class library) as topics for research, reports, written papers, or as topics for guest speakers.

2. Have a Missouri Day during which you learn about the state of Missouri. Have students research the geography, famous people from Missouri, industry, cities, things to see and do in Missouri, etc.

3. Discuss Muff Potter as an example of trouble springing from alcohol abuse.

4. Have students design a book cover (front and back and inside flaps) for *The Adventures of Tom Sawyer*.

5. Have students design a bulletin board (ready to be put up; not just sketched) for *The Adventures of Tom Sawyer*.

6. Have a treasure hunt. Make paper "treasures" that represent prizes the students will win when they find the "treasures." (Use the paper instead of the actual treasure because someone else from another class might come along and snatch up the real treasure whereas they would be less likely to move your paper "treasure.") Hide the treasures at different places on your school grounds. Give specific written directions about how to find each item. ("Go out the door and turn right. At the third set of lockers, turn left. Go to the water fountain by the stairs and walk through the double doors. Etc.) This is an exercise in following directions.

7. Have students compose a rap song or a ballad about the adventures of Tom Sawyer (as a review of the main ideas and events in the story).

8. Do a group writing assignment in which students compose the plot for an additional adventure for Tom Sawyer (as a check of their knowledge of the character of Tom and his motivations).

9. Have students rewrite the story from Aunt Polly's point of view -- perhaps as a letter from Aunt Polly to a friend "back East" relating the events that have been going on in her life.

WORD SEARCH - *The Adventures of Tom Sawyer*

All words in this list are associated with *The Adventures of Tom Sawyer*. The words are placed backwards, forward, diagonally, up and down. The included words are listed below the word searches.

```
V W J S K Q N P K Q R C P K N T T D R T H X C H
P W Q O R W S R P Y D N A I N T I O E H O C T R
K N I F E N A M H S L E W T R A P P E D M M O M
P N B T I B U L O B B L L U S A A Y S D A B V Q
K B O A C R T F T K N E O D N I T P D R I R C H
P K W S D H G W I E E C C P N J N E Y N G C T L
J T B E K R E F O N R T S K E A K J S E D A P S
Y G R O E C F S E J N S I R Y C C O U I F I N E
V T O T L I A W Q B E L U Y U D N S S N N W C G
S B T C K G S J D N L S M H C R F T Q C T N S C
H O U S E P S W T E A A R W E F I S H E E G E N
P Z V M A N E I R E R E W H U C U B C I I V J Z
M L Y P I L W T R P Y F C C L J U N C W A Z L W
Z Q E B V J G T E W K T L T F G E S E C Z H Q K
N R B W J H N U A R A Y L A Y F N V R R T F D N
N O G Q Y V H S O H L G Z N W O G R Q F A N C F
D C L E M E N S T D S T E K C I T B D R J L Q G
```

ALFRED	FENCE	NEWSPAPER	THATCHER
AMY	FINN	PAINKILLER	TICKETS
BARK	FISH	PETER	TOE
BECKY	FUNERAL	PINCHBUG	TOM
BOOK	GANG	PIRATES	TRADED
CANDLE	HOUSE	POLLY	TRAPPED
CATS	HUCK	POTTER	TREASURE
CAVE	INJUN	ROBINSON	TWAIN
CLEMENS	INK	SAWYER	TWO
CONSCIENCE	JACKSON	SID	WALTERS
COURT	JOE	SKIFF	WELSHMAN
CUFFS	KNIFE	SMOKE	WIG
DOBBINS	MARY	SPADE	WITCHES
DOUGLAS	MURDER	SPIT	WITNESS

KEY: WORD SEARCH - *The Adventures of Tom Sawyer*

All words in this list are associated with *The Adventures of Tom Sawyer*. The words are placed backwards, forward, diagonally, up and down. The included words are listed below the word searches.

```
            J           K       C P       T T D     T
        W   O   W S R   Y       A I     T I O E   O         R
    K N I F E N A M H S L E W T R A P P E D   M O
        N   T I B U L O   B L L U S A A   S   A B
    K   O A C R T F T K   E O D   I T       R I R
        W S D H   W I E E C C P N   N E Y N G     T
    T   E K R E F O N R   S K E A K J S E D A P S
        R O E C F S E   N S I R Y C C O U I   I N E
        O T   I A W     E L U Y U   N S S N N   C G
    B T     K   S J D N L S M H   R F       C   N
H O U S E P S       T E A A R   E F I S H E E G E
P           A N E I R E R E   H U   U B C I I V
            P I L W T R   Y F C C       U N C W A
    E   B       G T E W   T L     G E S E C
R   B             U A R A     A   F N     R
O                 S O H           O       A
D C L E M E N S T D S T E K C I T               L
```

ALFRED	FENCE	NEWSPAPER	THATCHER
AMY	FINN	PAINKILLER	TICKETS
BARK	FISH	PETER	TOE
BECKY	FUNERAL	PINCHBUG	TOM
BOOK	GANG	PIRATES	TRADED
CANDLE	HOUSE	POLLY	TRAPPED
CATS	HUCK	POTTER	TREASURE
CAVE	INJUN	ROBINSON	TWAIN
CLEMENS	INK	SAWYER	TWO
CONSCIENCE	JACKSON	SID	WALTERS
COURT	JOE	SKIFF	WELSHMAN
CUFFS	KNIFE	SMOKE	WIG
DOBBINS	MARY	SPADE	WITCHES
DOUGLAS	MURDER	SPIT	WITNESS

CROSSWORD - *The Adventures of Tom Sawyer*

CROSSWORD CLUES - *The Adventures of Tom Sawyer*

ACROSS

2. Huck's last name
4. Cat
7. Tom blew out Becky's to conserve
8. _____'s Island
10. A gory one was found next to Dr. Robinson
14. AKA Mark Twain
17. One only
18. Past tense of 'to be'
19. Injun Joe --- in the cave
20. The boys left it and the pick downstairs
23. Tom had been engaged to her before Becky
26. Number ___
27. Huck, Tom and Joe -- or any three together
28. Place where the trial is held
30. Becky tore the teacher's
31. Place where Tom and Becky got lost
32. He took the blame for tearing the teacher's book
34. Tom could do this through the gap in his teeth
36. Part of your face under your mouth
38. Tom's notepaper
39. The boys stole Mr. Dobbins's
40. Belonging to him
41. Huck taught Tom and Joe how to do this bad habit
42. Haunted ____
44. Tom got these and kisses from Aunt Polly upon his return
46. Tom passed time in church by watching this
47. Tom's guardian
48. Ten yellow ones were redeemed for a Bible
49. You have to dig for it where the shadow of a dead tree limb falls at midnight
50. Small boat
51. New boy; spilled ink on Tom's book

DOWN

1. _____ Joe; murderer
2. Tom was supposed to whitewash it
3. It spilled on Tom's spelling book
5. Tom had a sore one
6. Doctor Injun Joe killed
7. Dead ones are good for curing warts
8. Went to island with Huck and Tom
9. Tom's last name
11. Tom's name was printed in it for telling on Injun Joe
12. Food for island boys
13. Tom brought things to Muff Potter to ease his ____
15. Tom's girl cousin
16. Tom's half-brother
21. Teacher
22. Son of the town drunk
24. What Tom and Huck witnessed in the graveyard
25. Injun Joe got ____ in the cave and died
26. Becky's last name
29. Group of boys; Tom Sawyer's ____
33. The river
35. Author
37. The Widow
38. Engaged to Tom
42. Huck has a bad --- of smoking
43. They wore fancy clothes
45. The boys attended their own
46. Muff; drunk accused of murder

CROSSWORD ANSWER KEY - *The Adventures of Tom Sawyer*

MATCHING QUIZ/WORKSHEET 1 - *The Adventures of Tom Sawyer*

___ 1. DOUGLAS   A. Place where the trial is held

___ 2. TOE   B. How Tom got his tickets

___ 3. WALTERS   C. Tom's notepaper

___ 4. POLLY   D. You have to dig for it where the shadow of a dead tree limb falls at midnight

___ 5. DOBBINS   E. It spilled on Tom's spelling book

___ 6. SID   F. Author

___ 7. BARK   G. Tom blew out Becky's to conserve

___ 8. TREASURE   H. Tom gave some to Peter, making his act crazy

___ 9. ALFRED   I. Tom's half-brother

___ 10. CANDLE   J. Becky tore the teacher's

___ 11. POTTER   K. Muff; drunk accused of murder

___ 12. TWAIN   L. Tom's guardian

___ 13. PAINKILLER   M. The Widow

___ 14. TRADED   N. Tom had a sore one

___ 15. BOOK   O. Tom passed time in church by watching this

___ 16. PINCHBUG   P. Tom brought things to Muff Potter to ease his

___ 17. CONSCIENCE   Q. Teacher

___ 18. COURT   R. Sunday school superintendent

___ 19. THATCHER   S. Becky's last name

___ 20. INK   T. New boy; spilled ink on Tom's book

KEY: MATCHING QUIZ/WORKSHEET 1 - *The Adventures of Tom Sawyer*

M 1. DOUGLAS   A. Place where the trial is held

N 2. TOE   B. How Tom got his tickets

R 3. WALTERS   C. Tom's notepaper

L 4. POLLY   D. You have to dig for it where the shadow of a dead tree limb falls at midnight

Q 5. DOBBINS   E. It spilled on Tom's spelling book

I 6. SID   F. Author

C 7. BARK   G. Tom blew out Becky's to conserve

D 8. TREASURE   H. Tom gave some to Peter, making his act crazy

T 9. ALFRED   I. Tom's half-brother

G 10. CANDLE   J. Becky tore the teacher's

K 11. POTTER   K. Muff; drunk accused of murder

F 12. TWAIN   L. Tom's guardian

H 13. PAINKILLER   M. The Widow

B 14. TRADED   N. Tom had a sore one

J 15. BOOK   O. Tom passed time in church by watching this

O 16. PINCHBUG   P. Tom brought things to Muff Potter to ease his

P 17. CONSCIENCE   Q. Teacher

A 18. COURT   R. Sunday school superintendent

S 19. THATCHER   S. Becky's last name

E 20. INK   T. New boy; spilled ink on Tom's book

MATCHING QUIZ/WORKSHEET 2 - *The Adventures of Tom Sawyer*

___ 1. WELSHMAN   A. Tom's town

___ 2. CANDLE   B. Tom was supposed to whitewash it

___ 3. DOBBINS   C. Place where Tom and Becky got lost

___ 4. MURDER   D. Tom had a sore one

___ 5. INK   E. Number ___

___ 6. PAINKILLER   F. The Widow

___ 7. TOE   G. Went to island with Huck and Tom

___ 8. FENCE   H. It spilled on Tom's spelling book

___ 9. THATCHER   I. Tom blew out Becky's to conserve

___ 10. PIRATES   J. Author

___ 11. DOUGLAS   K. He saved Widow Douglas

___ 12. MARY   L. Tom's girl cousin

___ 13. TWO   M. Teacher

___ 14. CAVE   N. They wore fancy clothes

___ 15. TWAIN   O. Tom's notepaper

___ 16. ST. PETERSBURG   P. AKA Mark Twain

___ 17. JOE   Q. Tom's half-brother

___ 18. SID   R. What Tom and Huck witnessed in the graveyard

___ 19. BARK   S. Tom gave some to Peter, making him act crazy

___ 20. CLEMENS   T. Becky's last name

KEY: MATCHING QUIZ/WORKSHEET 2 - *The Adventures of Tom Sawyer*

K   1. WELSHMAN   A. Tom's town

I   2. CANDLE   B. Tom was supposed to whitewash it

M   3. DOBBINS   C. Place where Tom and Becky got lost

R   4. MURDER   D. Tom had a sore one

H   5. INK   E. Number ___

S   6. PAINKILLER   F. The Widow

D   7. TOE   G. Went to island with Huck and Tom

B   8. FENCE   H. It spilled on Tom's spelling book

T   9. THATCHER   I. Tom blew out Becky's to conserve

N   10. PIRATES   J. Author

F   11. DOUGLAS   K. He saved Widow Douglas

L   12. MARY   L. Tom's girl cousin

E   13. TWO   M. Teacher

C   14. CAVE   N. They wore fancy clothes

J   15. TWAIN   O. Tom's notepaper

A   16. ST.PETERSBURG   P. AKA Mark Twain

G   17. JOE   Q. Tom's half-brother

Q   18. SID   R. What Tom and Huck witnessed in the graveyard

O   19. BARK   S. Tom gave some to Peter, making him act crazy

P   20. CLEMENS   T. Becky's last name

JUGGLE LETTER REVIEW GAME CLUE SHEET - *The Adventures of Tom Sawyer*

SCRAMBLED	WORD	CLUE
ETO	TOE	Tom had a sore one
DDTERA	TRADED	How Tom got his tickets
ETDAPPR	TRAPPED	Injun Joe got _____ in the cave and died
SCEWTIH	WITCHES	Tom blamed the unsuccessful marble spell on these
CSKTTEI	TICKETS	Ten yellow ones were redeemed for a Bible
FSFIK	SKIFF	Small boat
UFCSF	CUFFS	Tom got these and kisses from Aunt Polly upon his return
RMYA	MARY	Tom's girl cousin
KRAB	BARK	Tom's notepaper
ACST	CATS	Dead ones are good for curing warts
REMRDU	MURDER	What Tom and Huck witnessed in the graveyard
OBKO	BOOK	Becky tore the teacher's
OTW	TWO	Number _____
NIRLIALEKP	PAINKILLER	Tom gave some to Peter, making him act crazy
YLOPL	POLLY	Tom's guardian
YAM	AMY	Tom had been engaged to her before Becky
SSSPMIIIIPS	MISSISSIPPI	The river
RRESETAU	TREASURE	You have to dig for it where the shadow of a dead tree limb falls at midnight
DSI	SID	Tom's half-brother
JUNNI	INJUN	_____ Joe; murderer
FKNEI	KNIFE	A gory one was found next to Dr. Robinson
OPRTTE	POTTER	Muff; drunk accused of murder
SCENCCENOI	CONSCIENCE	Tom brought things to Muff Potter to ease his _____
OSNBNIRO	ROBINSON	Doctor Injun Joe killed
EREPT	PETER	Cat
ALSOUGD	DOUGLAS	The Widow
OEMSK	SMOKE	Huck taught Tom and Joe how to do this bad habit
SWRELTA	WALTERS	Sunday school superintendent
LARFEUN	FUNERAL	The boy attended their own
TIPS	SPIT	Tom could do this through the gap in his teeth
TRAPESI	PIRATES	They wore fancy clothes
HMWNAELS	WELSHMAN	He saved Widow Douglas
OEJ	JOE	Went with Tom and Huck to the island

VOCABULARY RESOURCE MATERIALS

VOCABULARY WORD SEARCH - *The Adventures of Tom Sawyer*

All words in this list are associated with *The Adventures of Tom Sawyer* with an emphasis on the vocabulary words chosen for study in the text. The words are placed backwards, forward, diagonally, up and down. The included words are listed below.

```
W N X N N S D F L G E Z R V D Z F W J W X W N L
M J O L S G T V W T N N A E M Y G E A C A O H D
D E R I S I O N O I T I R T T A L A C R I T Y P
M E L A T P M M E E N U T E N B S O Y T I L D G
C B O A E U S P V S T Z D A I E U S A K B L V L
M H S C N S L O E A N I A S T N U C E A D S Y V
R J A U S C C O C R O O U W T I I Q I N U J D Q
C B B O B E H I S U I A C E E L G R O O T W V H
P O L A S D R O S E L S N D P D A O I L E R S G
I E N N B A U F L P R A H P I V E N C C E T P Z
H M R D C A L E J Y N E U A N L E V I E S S R N
O A P P E A S E D C N S R I B G L V I E A L P H
C D C A L S P H E Z S P A O N L S A U R A S Y H
H D I J I E C C E K U D X I L W E Q P U T B E C
T R S O P R X E D D S X W G Q P N P T B Q N Y D
Y G H R U L E E N I A T S B A I M U N K X L O W
L H Y T K S V D D D E T R E V A M I C T F H J C
```

ABASHED	COGITATING	IMPLORE	SMOTE
ABSTAIN	CONDESCEND	INGENIOUS	SUBDUED
ALACRITY	CONSENT	INQUESTS	SUPPLICATION
APPEASED	CONTRIVED	INVARIABLY	TEDIOUS
ASSENT	COUNTENANCE	MELANCHOLY	VAIN
ATTRITION	COVET	MUTUAL	VICE
AVERTED	DERISION	ODIOUS	WARILY
AWED	DISDAIN	PALLID	WARY
BLISS	ELOQUENT	PERPLEXED	CEASED
CARICATURE	FRESCOED	PLAUSIBLE	SEAR
IMPAIRED	RESOLUTION	CHAOS	IMPERISHABLE

KEY: VOCABULARY WORD SEARCH - *The Adventures of Tom Sawyer*

All words in this list are associated with *The Adventures of Tom Sawyer* with an emphasis on the vocabulary words chosen for study in the text. The words are placed backwards, forward, diagonally, up and down. The included words are listed below.

```
        N       S         G E     V         W         W N
    M   O   S   T       T N   A E         E A     A O
    D E R I S I O N O I T I R T T A L A C R I T Y
      E L A T   M M E E N U T E N B S O Y T I L
    C B O A E U S P V S T   D A I E U S A   B L
      H S C N S L O E A N I A S T N U C E A   S Y
        A U S C C O C R O O U W T I I Q I N U
    C     O B E H I S U I A C E E L G R O O T
    P O   A S D R O S E L S N D P D A O I L E   S
    I E N   B A U F L P R A H P I V E N C C E T
      M R D C A   E   Y N E U A N L E V I E S
    O A P P E A S E D C   S R I B G L V I E A L
      D   A L S   H E     P A O N L   A U R A S
          I   I E C   E   U D   I L   E Q P U T     E
            O   R X E   D S       P N   T     N   D
              U   E E N I A T S B A I M U       O
                S   D D D E T R E V A M I           C
```

ABASHED	COGITATING	IMPLORE	SMOTE
ABSTAIN	CONDESCEND	INGENIOUS	SUBDUED
ALACRITY	CONSENT	INQUESTS	SUPPLICATION
APPEASED	CONTRIVED	INVARIABLY	TEDIOUS
ASSENT	COUNTENANCE	MELANCHOLY	VAIN
ATTRITION	COVET	MUTUAL	VICE
AVERTED	DERISION	ODIOUS	WARILY
AWED	DISDAIN	PALLID	WARY
BLISS	ELOQUENT	PERPLEXED	CEASED
CARICATURE	FRESCOED	PLAUSIBLE	SEAR
IMPAIRED	RESOLUTION	CHAOS	IMPERISHABLE

VOCABULARY CROSSWORD - The Adventures of Tom Sawyer

VOCABULARY CROSSWORD CLUES - *The Adventures of Tom Sawyer*

ACROSS
1. Bad habit
4. Becky's last name
7. Stopped
9. Doctor Injun Joe killed
10. Huck's last name
11. Difficult to bear
12. Burn; scorch
15. Engaged to Tom
17. Is able to
18. Becky tore the teacher's
20. Also
21. The boys tell little white ones; fibs
24. Agree to something
25. Tom had a sore one
26. Anxiously
28. Tom's half-brother
29. Inflicted a heavy blow upon
31. The boys stole Mr. Dobbins's
32. Coordinating conjunction
33. Amazed with mixed emotions of reverence, respect and dread
34. Missouri or Mississippi, for example
35. Eagerness
39. Cautiously
40. Fearless
41. Tom had been engaged to her before Becky
44. Arousing a strong dislike or displeasure
47. Ashamed; uneasy; disconcerted
49. Beg
50. A gradual rubbing away or wearing down
51. A gory one was found next to Dr. Robinson

DOWN
1. Excessively proud
2. Disorder; confusion
3. Ridicule
4. Number ___
5. After Muff's ---- was presented to the judge
6. New boy; spilled ink on Tom's book
7. Drawing in which the subject's distinctive traits are exaggerated
8. Agreement
9. Determination
13. Turned away
14. Lower oneself to the position of inferiors
16. Went to island with Huck and Tom
19. It spilled on Tom's spelling book
22. The boys left it and the pick downstairs
23. Extreme happiness
24. Thinking
25. A ruler's unjust use of power
26. Calmed; satisfied; pacified
27. A chicken lays one
30. Possessed in common
31. Cautious
36. Stop doing something by one's own choice
37. He took the blame for tearing the teacher's book
38. Contempt
42. Want
43. Tom's notepaper
45. Cease; end; halt
46. Acquire; Tom and Huck --- the money
48. Injun Joe ---s in the cave

VOCABULARY CROSSWORD ANSWER KEY - *The Adventures of Tom Sawyer*

VOCABULARY WORKSHEET 1 - *The Adventures of Tom Sawyer*

___ 1. AVERTED   A. stop doing something by one's own choice

___ 2. TYRANNY   B. dangerously lacking in security or stability

___ 3. PRECARIOUS   C. courageously noble

___ 4. MAGNANIMOUS   D. face

___ 5. PERPLEXED   E. anxiously

___ 6. COVET   F. stimulated; sharpened

___ 7. IMPERISHABLE   G. lower oneself to the position of inferiors

___ 8. APPREHENSIVELY   H. amazed with mixed emotions or reverence, respect and dread

___ 9. WHETTED   I. puzzled; uncertain

___ 10. SEAR   J. pale; dull; lifeless

___ 11. WARILY   K. turned away

___ 12. COUNTENANCE   L. agree to something

___ 13. CONSENT   M. indestructible

___ 14. AWED   N. burn; scorch

___ 15. ELOQUENT   O. clever, inventive

___ 16. INGENIOUS   P. cautiously

___ 17. IMPAIRED   Q. characterized by persuasive, powerful or moving discourse

___ 18. CONDESCEND   R. damaged, diminished in strength

___ 19. ABSTAIN   S. want

___ 20. PALLID   T. a ruler's unjust use of power

KEY: VOCABULARY WORKSHEET 1 - *The Adventures of Tom Sawyer*

K 1. AVERTED   A. stop doing something by one's own choice

T 2. TYRANNY   B. dangerously lacking in security or stability

B 3. PRECARIOUS   C. courageously noble

C 4. MAGNANIMOUS   D. face

I 5. PERPLEXED   E. anxiously

S 6. COVET   F. stimulated; sharpened

M 7. IMPERISHABLE   G. lower oneself to the position of inferiors

E 8. APPREHENSIVELY   H. amazed with mixed emotions or reverence, respect and dread

F 9. WHETTED   I. puzzled; uncertain

N 10. SEAR   J. pale; dull; lifeless

P 11. WARILY   K. turned away

D 12. COUNTENANCE   L. agree to something

L 13. CONSENT   M. indestructible

H 14. AWED   N. burn; scorch

Q 15. ELOQUENT   O. clever, inventive

O 16. INGENIOUS   P. cautiously

R 17. IMPAIRED   Q. characterized by persuasive, powerful or moving discourse

G 18. CONDESCEND   R. damaged, diminished in strength

A 19. ABSTAIN   S. want

J 20. PALLID   T. a ruler's unjust use of power

VOCABULARY WORKSHEET 2 - *The Adventures of Tom Sawyer*

___ 1. Ridicule
    a. Derision   b. Frescoed   c. Upbraid   d. Perplexed

___ 2. Stopped
    a. Imperishable   b. Ceased   c. Vice   d. Sear

___ 3. Without change
    a. Countenance   b. Invariably   c. Pervading   d. Magnanimous

___ 4. Judicial inquiry into the cause of a death
    a. Appeased   b. Odious   c. Inquests   d. Contrived

___ 5. Beg
    a. Apprehensively   b. Implore   c. Derision   d. Inquests

___ 6. Agreement
    a. Upbraid   b. Bliss   c. Assent   d. Attrition

___ 7. Ashamed; uneasy; disconcerted
    a. Magnanimous   b. Abashed   c. Implore   d. Prodigious

___ 8. Difficult to bear
    a. Inquests   b. Oppressive   c. Dauntless   d. Sear

___ 9. Lower oneself to the position of inferiors
    a. Appeased   b. Consent   c. Condescend   d. Derision

___ 10. Present throughout
    a. Awed   b. Pervading   c. Supplication   d. Chaos

___ 11. Schemed
    a. Contrived   b. Unpalatable   c. Cogitating   d. Tyranny

___ 12. Possessed in common
    a. Mutual   b. Disdain   c. Dauntless   d. Abashed

___ 13. Arousing a strong dislike or displeasure
    a. Condescend   b. Melancholy   c. Mutual   d. Odious

___ 14. Face
    a. Countenance   b. Ingenious   c. Tedious   d. Pervading

___ 15. Want
    a. Odious   b. Precipice   c. Covet   d. Precarious

___ 16. Indestructible
    a. Averted   b. Chaos   c. Imperishable   d. Tedious

___ 17. Cautious
    a. Attrition   b. Vain   c. Plausible   d. Wary

___ 18. Puzzled; uncertain
    a. Implore   b. Frescoed   c. Averted   d. Perplexed

___ 19. Reprimand
    a. Condescend   b. Bliss   c. Upbraid   d. Prodigious

___ 20. Drawing in which the subject's distinctive traits are exaggerated
    a. Prodigious   b. Caricature   c. Whetted   d. Pervading

KEY: VOCABULARY WORKSHEET 2 - *The Adventures of Tom Sawyer*

__A__ 1. Ridicule
    a. Derision   b. Frescoed   c. Upbraid   d. Perplexed

__B__ 2. Stopped
    a. Imperishable   b. Ceased   c. Vice   d. Sear

__B__ 3. Without change
    a. Countenance   b. Invariably   c. Pervading   d. Magnanimous

__C__ 4. Judicial inquiry into the cause of a death
    a. Appeased   b. Odious   c. Inquests   d. Contrived

__B__ 5. Beg
    a. Apprehensively   b. Implore   c. Derision   d. Inquests

__C__ 6. Agreement
    a. Upbraid   b. Bliss   c. Assent   d. Attrition

__B__ 7. Ashamed; uneasy; disconcerted
    a. Magnanimous   b. Abashed   c. Implore   d. Prodigious

__B__ 8. Difficult to bear
    a. Inquests   b. Oppressive   c. Dauntless   d. Sear

__C__ 9. Lower oneself to the position of inferiors
    a. Appeased   b. Consent   c. Condescend   d. Derision

__B__ 10. Present throughout
    a. Awed   b. Pervading   c. Supplication   d. Chaos

__A__ 11. Schemed
    a. Contrived   b. Unpalatable   c. Cogitating   d. Tyranny

__A__ 12. Possessed in common
    a. Mutual   b. Disdain   c. Dauntless   d. Abashed

__D__ 13. Arousing a strong dislike or displeasure
    a. Condescend   b. Melancholy   c. Mutual   d. Odious

__A__ 14. Face
    a. Countenance   b. Ingenious   c. Tedious   d. Pervading

__C__ 15. Want
    a. Odious   b. Precipice   c. Covet   d. Precarious

__C__ 16. Indestructible
    a. Averted   b. Chaos   c. Imperishable   d. Tedious

__D__ 17. Cautious
    a. Attrition   b. Vain   c. Plausible   d. Wary

__D__ 18. Puzzled; uncertain
    a. Implore   b. Frescoed   c. Averted   d. Perplexed

__C__ 19. Reprimand
    a. Condescend   b. Bliss   c. Upbraid   d. Prodigious

__B__ 20. Drawing in which the subject's distinctive traits are exaggerated
    a. Prodigious   b. Caricature   c. Whetted   d. Pervading

VOCABULARY JUGGLE LETTER REVIEW GAME CLUES - *The Adventures of Tom Sawyer*

SCRAMBLED	WORD	CLUE
LEHIIEPMBSAR	IMPERISHABLE	Indestructible
TEETWDH	WHETTED	Stimulated; sharpened
DEWA	AWED	Amazed with mixed emotions of reverence, respect and dread
UGDISIPOOR	PRODIGIOUS	Impressively great
SADNIID	DISDAIN	Contempt
HASCO	CHAOS	Disorder; confusion
OSODIU	ODIOUS	Arousing a strong dislike or displeasure
LBSSI	BLISS	Extreme happiness
STBANAI	ABSTAIN	Stop doing something by one's own choice
OSENTIRLUO	RESOLUTION	Determination
CISOTPNUPAIL	SUPPLICATION	A plea
SCDCEENDON	CONDESCEND	Lower oneself to the position of inferiors
DDSUEUB	SUBDUED	Conquered and brought under control; quieted
UNIINESOG	INGENIOUS	Clever; inventive
PSREOVEPIS	OPPRESSIVE	Difficult to bear
NGOASMAINMU	MAGNANIMOUS	Courageously noble
RESOEFDC	FRESCOED	Painted
OTESM	SMOTE	Inflicted a heavy blow upon
IVNA	VAIN	Excessively proud
YRANYTN	TYRANNY	A ruler's unjust use of power
SULEAPLIB	PLAUSIBLE	Believable
RASE	SEAR	Burn; scorch
AARTCLYI	ALACRITY	Eagerness
ETDVAER	AVERTED	Turned away
EPXRDPELE	PERPLEXED	Puzzled; uncertain
TINICGGOAT	COGITATING	Thinking
NPAERVGDI	PERVADING	Present throughout
ABLINAIYRV	INVARIABLY	Without change
RDAMIEIP	IMPAIRED	Damaged; diminished in strength
ALTEBLUNAAP	UNPALATABLE	Unacceptable to the mind or senses
YLAWIR	WARILY	Cautiously
LLAIDP	PALLID	Pale; dull; lifeless
TVECO	COVET	Want
IIPCERCEP	PRECIPICE	Overhanging rock; cliff
UETNQSIS	INQUESTS	Judicial inquiry into the cause of a death
ESTNSA	ASSENT	Agreement
IBAURDP	UPBRAID	Reprimand